Everything I Know About Widowhood I Learned From Jessica Fletcher

Christina Hamlett

Published by Christina Hamlett, 2024.

EVERYTHING I KNOW ABOUT WIDOWHOOD I LEARNED FROM JESSICA FLETCHER

First edition. February 27, 2024.

ISBN: 979-8224891276

Written by Christina Hamlett.

Table of Contents

To Cindy, Liz, Maureen and Millie whose love and courage
were a bright beacon for me to follow.

To Abby, Candice, Gracie, Jon, Barb, Jamie, Tari, Rachel,
Jeremy, Lauren, Rose, Saul, Joanna, Bill, Carolyn, Marlise,
Laura, Michael, Vicki and Chaplin Charly whose phone calls,
emails and hugs encouraged me beyond words.

And to Peter for inventing Jessica.

WHY JESSICA FLETCHER?

Total strangers often comment I don't seem to have aged very much despite the passage of decades. My response is to tell them that—along with good genes—I have a hideous portrait of myself tucked up in the attic which does the aging *for* me.

If I say this to anyone under the age of 30, however, they typically look confused, say "Huh?" and ask why I have a hideous portrait at all. Good heavens but are they no longer teaching the classics in high school that my reference to Oscar Wilde's *The Picture of Dorian Gray* would go completely over their heads?

The transitory nature of modern pop culture—and especially television—compels me to take into account that future readers of this book may have no clue as to who Jessica Fletcher was, much less any passing familiarity with the TV series which brought her plucky amateur sleuth persona into households every Sunday evening going back to 1984.

When I first shared on social media that I was writing this book, someone said, "Ooooh, this sounds really good. Are we going to find out who Jessica Fletcher is?"

I rest my case.

From the first time I saw *Murder, She Wrote*, I was instantly hooked. That it starred one of my favorite actresses, Angela Lansbury, was just frosting on the cake. (Die-hard movie buffs may recall that Ms. Lansbury played the tragically lovelorn Sibyl Vane in the 1945 adaptation of Wilde's novel.) Every week, I'd watch the name of the show's creator, Peter S. Fischer, scroll up the credits and be amazed at how prolific he was. (He also wrote the scripts for *Columbo* on the very same typewriter I was gifted with after his retirement.)

I had no idea that 26 years after the debut of MSW, my husband and I would become good friends with Peter and his lovely wife, Lucille. No trip to California's Monterey Peninsula was ever complete without having lunch with the two of them at Fandango and having Peter regale us with stories about working with "Angie" and the cast of fictional characters who consistently made Cabot Cove (Maine) the unofficial Murder Capital of the World.

Nor could I have envisioned that 13 years after we met Peter, I would be drawing strength and inspiration from his fictional J.B. Fletcher to help me cope with one of the most devastating events of my life: the unexpected death of my beloved husband, Mark, from Stage 4 cancer.

He was perfectly fine during the holidays but in January started having problems keeping food down. The irony of this is that both of us are gourmet chefs and Mark in particular was quite the expert on wine pairings. For several years on Facebook we posted something every Monday called *Culinary Capers* in which we'd alternate trying new recipes from our 300+ cookbooks and subscriptions to *Gourmet* and *Food & Wine*.

Friends and colleagues salivated every week in anticipation of what we two would cook up next. Between my photography skills and his enthusiasm to share tips, shortcuts and substitutions, nothing was more gratifying than to hear fans tell us they had replicated our efforts in their own homes for family and guests.

The last "normal" meals we enjoyed together at our dining table were Christmas Day and New Year's in 2022. Shortly thereafter, he began pushing his plate away and declining refills of wine. Fatigue was showing in everything he was doing and he seemed agitated and short-tempered about the simplest tasks. I knew he wasn't angry at me and yet, to be honest, it was a challenge not to take it that way and respond in kind.

We had talked about taking a trip for our 25th anniversary but the enthusiasm he'd had for our past travels just didn't seem to be there. He brightened briefly when I reminded him he had always wanted to take me to the Fairmont Empress in Victoria, British Columbia. Throughout our time together, we had shared a love of grand old hotels, and the Empress would certainly meet that definition. I had already commenced the task of sussing out flights, making sure our passports were current and putting together a budget. That we both worked from home and were, thus, answerable to no one but ourselves meant we didn't even have to put in requests for vacation.

His voice may have said yes to my ideas but his eyes communicated a hopelessness and a distance I'd never seen before.

My promptings—even the gentle ones—were not well met.

Men can be notoriously stubborn when it comes to their own health. I swear that if one of Mark's legs had been gnawed off by a shark on a trip to Hawaii, he'd have said, "Oh, it's okay. I've still got the other one. I'll just hop around..."

His weight loss was subtle at first. And then it became alarmingly noticeable. This is a man who for all the years I knew him was between 225 and 240 pounds and looked as dashing in a tuxedo as he did in his full regalia Scottish kilt. He was even more of a clotheshorse than I was and had a full closet of expensive suits, French-cuff shirts and silk ties. Although working from home transitioned his weekday wardrobe to sweatpants and tee-shirts, he never missed an opportunity for "date nights" so we could both dress up.

The morning he got on the scale and told me he had dropped to 190, the tears he tried to hold back told me he was afraid. Neither of us could have predicted that by the end his weight would have dropped 25 pounds more and left him almost skeletal.

"Maybe I should see someone," he murmured.

When he finally conceded there could be something seriously wrong, he made an appointment with our primary care provider who subsequently referred him to a gastroenterologist. A colonoscopy and an endoscopy were ordered for the following week, a scenario which caused my beloved to quip that they may as well put him on a barbeque spit and rotate him around for the procedure. Subsequent tests and scans revealed the worst possible news.

Stage 4?! How was this even possible, I thought. WTF happened to stages 1, 2, and 3? Shouldn't there be some sort of glide path to get you used to impending disaster? His oncology team at the hospital was first-rate and even optimistic that with an aggressive treatment regimen of radiation and chemo, they'd be able to get him to remission and potentially buy him a few more years.

I, of course, began beating myself up that I should have urged him to get to the doctor sooner. I was assured the cancer had probably started much earlier while we were still living in California but that he had shown absolutely no symptoms which would warrant concern.

The immediate priority was to try to get him to put some weight back on so his system could withstand the rigor of the upcoming treatments. The nutritionists recommended protein drinks and fruit juices and all manner of broths. Yet even these failed to stay down for very long. I remember going to the store and sitting in my car in the parking lot and crying out of frustration that nothing was working. I didn't want him to see that I was falling apart and so I made sure I always composed myself before I went home.

Ever perky.

Ever plucky.

Ever optimistic that his condition would somehow turn around.

Ten radiation treatments and a grueling five-hour chemo later, the bottom fell out of our world with an end-of-life diagnosis that the cancer had spread so deeply throughout his stomach and esophagus there was nothing which could be done to eradicate it, much less slow it down and give us more time together.

At this point he was ensconced in a private room at St. Luke's Hospital and subsisting on nothing more than liquids and IVs. Trouper that he was, he had asked me to bring his laptop computer so he could notify all of his clients, shut down his consulting business, provide me with all of his passwords and put together a bill-paying matrix so I would know how to proceed with the finances he had expertly handled throughout our marriage.

I forced myself not to look at the *Do Not Resuscitate* band on his left wrist, a dark reminder he could leave me at any moment.

I was informed I'd need to find a hospice situation to accommodate his needs. "We're ready to discharge your husband this morning," one of the doctors informed me.

"To what and to where?" I asked.

This particular doctor—whose bedside manner left much to be desired—informed me Medicare would cover the cost of hospice at home and that I would be his designated caregiver. Two problems with that. The first is that our multi-story townhouse was not configured for home hospice. Secondly, Mark was adamant against dying in our own bed and my last memory being the sight of him carried down the stairs and out the door in a body bag. He knew the emotional and physical stress that caregiving would impose on me and he wanted to avoid it at all costs.

Thus, compounding the trauma of a dying spouse, I was tasked with making my own arrangements for his future care as well as facing a staggering medical bill for each additional day he was functionally taking up space at a facility which could no longer do anything for him. A suite in a New York hotel, I was certain, would cost far less than the bill I'd be looking at in the immediate future. A bewildering scenario for which I was completely unprepared.

On one of my many tearful drives between home and the hospital, I found myself reflecting on Angela Lansbury and an interview she had given *The Daily Mail* following the death of her husband, Peter Shaw.

"We had the perfect relationship. Not many people can say that," she told the media. "He was everything to me: we were partners at work as well as husband and wife and lovers. I don't know how we had such a long marriage, but the simple fact was that we were devoted to one another. We made all decisions jointly and we helped and supported each other constantly."

I smiled at the comparison to our own relationship. A dear friend once remarked, "Yours is the romance and marriage a lot of us wish we had." Mark, too, was my partner in everything I did along with being an excellent editor, proofreader, brainstormer, legal counsel, IT guy and personal cheering section. I felt as if I wasn't just losing one person but at least seven for all of the roles he fulfilled in my life.

Ms. Lansbury had subsequently revealed that she used work and keeping busy to help navigate her grief and staggering loss. "Suddenly it happens, and that special person is gone," she explained. "I said, 'All right, enough already. Get off your ass and start moving forward.'"

Although I'm the first to admit a part of me was in denial I'd be without my beloved in a matter of weeks or months, I also knew not only would my own work sustain me but that Mark would expect nothing less of me than to pursue even more fervently the career which had begun long before the two of us met.

His condition was such that he was not a candidate for Assisted Living, nor could he be admitted to Skilled Nursing. I dug in my heels at the hospital's pushiness to get him discharged. What were they going to do—wheel him to the curb in his hospital gown and wish him a nice day?

I made it clear he wasn't going *anywhere* until arrangements had been made which I could feel good about.

As will be dealt with in a later chapter about funeral directors, it's a shameless travesty about the way medical professionals can sometimes guilt us into doing things against our wishes when we are in our weakest and most vulnerable states. If there is any lesson to be learned from this book, it's to not let down your defenses.

Whether through the power of luck or prayer, I was fortunate to get a nurse's referral to a husband and wife who had been doing home hospice for several years. They just happened to have a bedroom available in their house and lived a scant ten minutes from me. Even better, I could take our sweet little dog, Lucy, who was confused as ever about where her daddy had gone off to.

The moment I walked into the house for the interview, my first thought was that the cost of private hospice care was going to be exorbitant. (The doctors originally estimated Mark could live for several months.) My second thought was that I'd just have to figure out *how* to pay for it in order to assure his comfort and well-being.

The place to which I had been referred could best be described as a McMansion adjacent to a golf course and nestled amidst wide, tree-lined streets with streams and pristine lakes. The bedroom in which Mark would be staying was beautifully decorated, had its own bathroom and he would not only be looked after by the couple themselves but also by visiting nurses and clergy.

After I signed the paperwork arranging for his discharge and transport from St. Luke's, I was walking down the driveway and said to myself, "Okay, Universe. If he only lives three more days, I will be accepting of it and move on."

He had been nothing less than insistent in extracting a promise I not go the route of a friend of ours who completely let herself go following her husband's death from a long illness. Although several years had already passed for her, she shut off contact with friends, didn't pursue the activities she had so enjoyed before and rarely even left the house.

This would definitely not be the mindset of the gregarious and well-grounded Jessica Fletcher, nor would it be mine.

"How did you find me such a beautiful place?' Mark asked me, his voice barely above a whisper as he looked around after getting settled into his cozy new environment.

It was one of the last conversations we ever had. By this time, he was losing the capacity to speak and to write. He was sleeping a lot and subsisting on tiny sips of Welch's grape juice. Lucy and I went to visit him twice a day—she laying at the foot of his bed and me just telling him about my day. I even sang to him, one of his favorite songs being "On My Own" from *Les Miserables*.

On Easter Sunday, the couple invited me to have an early dinner with them. I was finally getting ready to leave when the wife drew me aside. She asked me to forgive her if she was speaking out of turn. "Were you going to tell him you'll see him tomorrow?"

I told her that that's *exactly* what I was going to say.

As diplomatically as she could, she told me that patients who know they are dying can often get anxious and stressed when a loved one says they will be back the next day. "They're tired. They want to let go. But they feel they have an obligation to not let down the people they care about. Even in pain, they feel as if they need to stay around."

I asked her what I should say instead.

She told me I could tell Mark I knew he was tired and wanted to let go and that it was all right.

And so that's what I said. I kissed him and said goodnight and sweet dreams and Lucy and I went on our way.

An hour later, she called to tell me Mark had died peacefully in his sleep.

Several days later, I told her I regretted leaving when I did, that maybe I should have just stayed an hour longer in order to be with him.

"No," she told me. "It was the last selfless act of love your husband did for you. He didn't want you to be there at the end. And so he waited until, in his heart of hearts, he knew you and Lucy were safely home. Only then could he finally go Home himself."

I would always be his wife in memory.

But from that night forward, I was now his widow.

Having spent sixteen years of my life treading the boards and running a touring theatre company, I found myself comparing this experience to The Actor's Nightmare.

Specifically:

Polite anticipation ripples through the audience as they take a final glance at their programs. The houselights start to dim, the precursor of a rising curtain. Backstage is the palpable rush of adrenalin amongst costumed members of the cast. Everyone knows their marks and are ready. Everyone except you. Truth be told, you don't even know what play is being performed, much less your role in it.

There's a reason they call it The Actors Nightmare, the unsettling anomaly of not being in sync on Opening Night. Even worse, you can't even wake yourself up. Such form of paralysis has probably been going on since the time of Shakespeare, although actors at The Globe were probably more stressed that Will wouldn't finish scribbling their latest lines on parchment before it was time for them to emerge from the wings and say something brill.

You know you're the star of this new show and much is riding on your keen sense of timing and delivery. If only you could grab someone's attention—preferably someone who has played this same role before—and ask them what you're supposed to do. Why couldn't someone have just left a copy of the script laying on a chair so you could at least do a quick thumb-through to get the gist?

Unfortunately, nothing could have prepared me for becoming a solo act after years of performing as a team.

Welcome to the world of widowhood.

ONCE UPON A TIME

Over the years, I have often been asked to repeat the story of how Mark and I first met. The short response was that I had wished him into existence. The long version is—well, it's all more or less true.

There is a measure of truth to the adage that good things come to those who wait. What they don't bother to tell you, of course, is (1) how long, exactly, that wait is going to be, or (2) that it may take so long you will have forgotten what it was you were waiting *for* when it finally arrives. This is not unlike the variety of vague prophecies found in fortune cookies: it is nice to know that "You will come into a large inheritance" but it would be more helpful if it included the words "next Wednesday" or "on your 34th birthday."

After two divorces, I was tired of waiting for happiness to once more roll in my direction instead of bouncing around like a ball on a roulette wheel. What began optimistically enough with an older man who looked like Richard Burton started going off the rails within the first year and a half of dating.

The tumultuous relationship with "Dick" was steadily chipping away at my faith in the dream I could ever have more than a part-time, wishy-washy paramour. Dick, you see, had a hard time extricating himself from his estranged wife, Estelle. "It's just not a good time" became his standard reply every time I queried when, exactly, their break would be final.

"You'll never meet someone new," a good friend wisely opined, "as long as you're keeping yourself hopelessly attached to someone else."

While I knew she was right, there still lingered the anxiety of never meeting anyone at all. Thus reconciled to this somewhat drekky half-life until I could find the courage to break free, I decided to take advantage of an especially aggressive airfare war and go to Scotland.

It was my second trip to the U.K. The co-worker who decided to join me—and who shared the popular view that Dick was a jerk—saw it as a chance to research her ancestry and maybe even catch a glimpse of the *Braveheart* and *Rob Roy* film crews. I saw it as an opportunity to not only contemplate the murky future but to give Dick plenty of time to miss me desperately and beg my return.

The first few days had been earmarked for sightseeing around London. "...and then I've blocked out all of Tuesday for a side-trip to Stonehenge and Bath," my traveling companion informed me.

Note to self: Never travel with an accountant who keeps a ledger book and wants both parties to zero out at the end of each day. Time and again she would try to foist additional drinks or desserts on me because, heaven forbid, our numbers weren't matching up.

It was a responsibility at which she excelled—planning every hour of our two-week itinerary down to the last angstrom of detail and price. Ordinarily such micro-managing behavior irritates the hell out of me, especially on vacation. Under the circumstances, though, I was content to let someone else do all the thinking and, thus, allow me to save valuable brain-space for thoughts of Dick. The fact she also volunteered to do all the driving and calculate the fluctuating exchange rate was just an added bonus.

Bath, for those of you unfamiliar with English history, dates back to the time of the Romans. What these early warriors may have lacked in terms of educational/literary pursuits was more than made up for by their ability to recognize a good party town when they found one. Bath—with its abundance of steaming mineral springs (rumored to yield strange and magical powers)—fit the bill for the perfect Roman Holiday.

Quicker than you could say "Et tu?", they erected what would be the forerunner of Club Med, along with a number of imposing statues of themselves around the perimeter so as to leave no question regarding authorship of the whole idea. Off came the togas, in came the tourists, and Bath today still looks pretty much like the Bath of yore except that the pool now resembles an inky-green Olympic-size petri dish which would probably dissolve anything that, literally, set foot in it.

Still, as English attractions go, it's not bad.

The point of this story, though—for those of you who were wondering if there was going to *be* one—involves the power of wishing.

It was just before lunch and our guide had directed us to the final stop on the tour of this ancient spa—an indoor well of water which, in the right light, resembled some giant community hot tub. "The legend," she explained, "says that anything asked for at this magic pool will come true."

She also whimsically added the postscript that The Pool Gods tended to favor those wishes accompanied by large denominations of coin. The larger, the better.

As I withdrew £2 from my purse, my traveling companion cautioned me to 'wish wisely'. Obviously she knew I was going to wish for Dick to come to his senses and make good on all of his romantic promises. "The problem with putting a specific name on a wish," she said, "is that it cuts out all the potential candidates who could meet what you think is some specialized criteria."

Fortunately, I was in a listening mood that day. I closed my eyes and made the request, "May a knight in shining armor be waiting for me when I get home and may our love and trust in one another be everlasting."

Kerplunk!

"So what did *you* wish for?" I asked my friend later on while we were having lunch.

She smiled. "I wished that Dick would get exactly what he deserves." Her exact words, to be honest, were, "I wish his dick falls off."

At the end of the day, these actually turned out to be the same thing.

Two Weeks Later...

To my dismay, there were only two messages on my machine from Dick when I got home. The first was to whine about how terribly he missed me and that he and Estelle were definitely going to be thinking of talking about maybe finally getting a divorce. The second was that they were going to Lake Tahoe on vacation but that he'd call when he got back.

My hope that absence would make the heart grow fonder turned out instead to be Out of Sight, Out of Mind.

I dragged myself into the office on Monday, still suffering the effects of jet lag and yet another punch in the heart. It was raining that day. I remember that because the next person who came through the door was wearing a western-style overcoat and hat which had seen recent sprinkles. What I noticed first, though, was that he had the kindest smile and a pair of blue eyes full of sparkle and life.

Apparently my eyes caught his attention as well and he complimented me on them. 'I hope you don't think this is forward of me to say, but you have the most beautiful eyes I've ever seen."

"And in that moment you said 'thank you," he later told me, "I felt as if I knew everything there was to know about you."

'Later', of course, is the operative word in this tale of love at first sight.

For nearly three years after that first hello, he'd stop by for impromptu meetings with the Department's director and various administrative officers. And each time, he'd linger at my desk a little longer. Oftentimes, he'd also bring a single truffle in a small white box from See's Candy, having once asked me what it would take to get a meeting with someone and being told, "I can be bribed with chocolate."

I had no idea his office was just one floor above ours. How *would* I, never having any occasion to go up there.

No matter what kind of day I was having, my spirits were always significantly lifted whenever the door opened and he walked in. I'd find myself saving up my funniest stories to share with him, just to prolong his being there. Whether or not anyone else noticed this pattern of flirtation, they didn't say.

Certainly from our own respective viewpoints, it was a habit which wasn't going to develop any further. I simply assumed a man as nice as this one was probably happily married. He assumed someone like me was taken as well. In fact, when I once shared with him I was taking my annual spring trip to Washington DC with a friend, he pictured me tucked away in a quaint B&B in Virginia with an adoring beau who looked like Tom Selleck. Little did he know I was referring to one of my gal pals who was a travel agent.

"So why did he never ask?" you may ask.

The bottom line is that Mark is a man who possessed more honor and integrity than anyone I have ever known. It wouldn't have been right, he later explained, to have a personal relationship with someone who worked in an office with which he had official business. The additional fact I might have said "no" would have made it all wonky and awkward in his subsequent visits to the office.

Things changed dramatically in February of 1997, owing to two major events.

The first was Valentine's Day.

I was still seeing Dick (was I stupid or what?) and still feeling miserable. "I'm bringing you a surprise at lunch," he promised. I found myself hoping it would be Estelle's head on a platter...or at least her name on divorce papers. Instead, he showed up with a pathetically scraggly bouquet of daisies and carnations in a vase of water which looked like it had come from Bath.

My first reaction was that he had my real flowers—preferably roses and a lot of them—behind his back. He didn't. He also seemed to read my mind. "You know how much they've jacked up the price of roses at the store?" he said. "It's criminal."

"It's Valentine's Day," I pointed out.

"Yeah, well I'm not gonna pay those kind of prices just for one stupid day that doesn't mean anything."

Apparently I didn't mean very much of anything, either.

And so there I sat all Friday afternoon with my limp-looking bouquet while delivery-after-delivery of breathtaking red roses arrived for all of my female co-workers. I didn't even have a romantic evening to look forward to. It was, after all, Valentine's Day which, according to Dick, was not one of those favored times to desert one's maniacal spouse.

At five minutes to five, the door opened and in walked Mark. "These are for you," he said, almost sheepishly, and handed me a small red box from See's containing not one but six of my favorite truffles.

What I didn't know—but had started to suspect—was that he was handing me more than a box of chocolate that day; he was handing me his heart.

I also didn't know that he, too, was going home to an empty house that evening. All I could really think about at the time was riding in a full elevator with a bunch of women who all had huge sprays of red roses...while I stood clutching my little red box and a bouquet of flowers which had already started to die.

The second event that month was that I got a promotion which meant a transfer out of downtown and into a field office. On the one hand, I was glad to escape the high cost of monthly parking; on the other hand, it was a move which put me closer to my favorite mall and the temptation to spend all the money I was supposed to be saving.

On yet another hand, I also realized I was going to miss the weekly truffle fix.

I saw him the day after I had accepted the job and boldly informed him that "choice dates are still available" to take me to lunch to celebrate the promotion. To my delight, he calendared one immediately. What I didn't know is that he went back to his office, jumped around in glee for a moment, and then went into panic at the prospect of spending an entire hour with this woman he had been secretly in love with since 1994.

Actually, it turned into much more than an hour. Three, to be precise—two hours and 55 minutes of which I spent yakking away out of nervousness. By the time he walked me back to the office, I was thinking, "Geez! Why did I have to talk so much? He'll never want to take me to lunch again."

While I was thinking those thoughts, he was thinking, "Wow! She sure likes to talk about herself a lot. I wonder what it would be like to be married to her and listen to that beautiful voice all the time…"

I had given him my new office number when we parted. "Maybe we can stay in touch," I said.

No one was more surprised than I was when he called me two weeks later to see how the job was going. "We could get together for a glass of wine sometime," I suggested.

"How about next week?" he replied.

The wine date proved to be yet another benchmark in our growing attraction, capped by my closing remark I hoped we'd always be "buddies."

Buddies????? Arghghghgh!

"I don't want to be her buddy!" his brain raged during his drive home. "I want to be her husband!"

The next time I heard from him was in April. Having remembered I am one of those people who blocks out the entire month for the purpose of celebrating my birthday, he called to see if "any choice dates" were still available to take me to lunch.

"As a matter of fact," I replied, "I'm free on The Day itself."

His first thought was "Yippee!" His second thought was, "Her birthday is on a Monday. If she's really dating Tom Selleck, why isn't he whisking her off for a long romantic weekend?" His keen Spidey senses began to spin and tell him that maybe, just *maybe* he had a chance.

I agreed to meet him at noon in the courtyard of The Firehouse, a popular restaurant in the historic sector of Sacramento. It's a good thing I had taken the day off, given that I changed dresses at least nine times that morning until finally settling on just the right one.

I arrived a few minutes before he did and, in fact, wasn't facing the courtyard gate when he entered. Almost as if knowing he was there, I turned at the precise moment he walked in.

Movie magic.

Think of Jane Seymour in *Somewhere in Time* when she turned to smile at Christopher Reeve while she was getting her picture taken. At least that's the sunlit memory indelibly locked in Mark's brain. He also knew at that very moment he couldn't leave the restaurant that day without declaring his feelings.

It was another three-hour lunch, at least an hour and a half of which was spent with neither one of us saying anything, just holding hands across the table and not wanting to ever let go.

He proposed to me that day and I accepted, the irony being we hadn't even exchanged our first kiss or had our first real date. It's also uncanny how many things we had in common—two percent milk, Crest toothpaste, loving dogs—in spite of never talking about any of these things during what is customarily the Q&A period of exploring a new relationship.

By the time we finally left The Firehouse, we had already determined we'd marry in a castle, honeymoon in the Scottish Highlands, and live happily ever after.

P.S. My friend's wish about Dick also came true. He is still with Estelle.

P.S.2. Remember I wished for a knight in shining armor? Well, the Romans apparently misheard one of the words I spoke that day. Shortly after Mark and I moved in together, he went into the office one weekend and came home with some items he thought would look nice in the condo. One of them was a 5' tall suit of armor he'd had for years and nicknamed Fred. Thus, readers, what I got was a knight *with* shining armor; a man who could fit *in* said suit of armor would be a tiny lad indeed.

P.S.3. For as long as we lived in Northern California and then Southern California, Fred steadfastly guarded the foot of the stairs. Now at Dobbs Mill, Fred guards the top of the staircase. I refer to him as our security system. Should any burglar ever be stupid enough to creep up the stairs at two in the morning, they will see a metal man in twilight with a sword and a plucky black raven named Edgar. And likely they will think, "Oh crap," and quietly let themselves out the front door and never return.

THE CONVERSATION

There are lots of conversations in life we'd just as soon not have. Many of them, I think, fall into the categories of facing our own fragile mortality or owning up to our loved ones that we have lived less than exemplary lives.

While no one likes to think about death and dying, it's ultimately far better to be prepared for the inevitable than to be caught unawares. For Mark and me, the first step in that process was having our wills drawn up.

In total candor, our primary reason was to ensure nothing would fall to his greedy piggy relatives in the event we both perished. Whether or not his mother and brother were aware of Mark's net worth, they for sure had no idea about mine—a mystery which fairly quickly became my mother-in-law's weird obsession to try to find out. Whenever we went on a vacation involving air travel, she'd always say, "I hope the two of you don't die in a horrible plane crash."

This, in fact, was probably the very thing she secretly hoped for. In the absence of any offspring on our part, she knew she and her son would be the only beneficiaries if there wasn't a will in place.

It was a fairly straightforward process for us to define who would get what, who would be assigned durable power of attorney, and who would be vested with health care directives in the event we weren't able to make such decisions for ourselves.

Left to his own devices, my beloved husband might not have mentioned such paperwork to them at all and let them continue to rub their hands together in the anticipatory glee of outliving us. That my own relationship with them was already deteriorating meant I wasn't bound by such constraints.

"So the good news," I declared in our weekly Sunday phone call, "is that Mark and I had our wills finalized."

My mother-in-law took the bait of asking what the bad news was.

"You and G aren't in it."

Mark caught the tail end of this conversation and said they'd probably never want to talk to me again.

Oh, if only.

"Do you think you'd remarry if something ever happened to me?"

Mark tended to ask this question more of me than I ever asked of him.

And so I'd pretend to ponder a bit and then rattle off names like Robert Downey, Jr., Tom Selleck, Colin Firth, Alan Rickman, Sean Bean, Johnny Depp, Hugh Jackman.

"You seem to have put a lot of thought into this," he'd say.

I reminded him that the Girl Scout motto was to Be Prepared.

His own list only had one name on it. Salma Hayek. Yet even in the next breath he told me if Salma threw herself naked into his path, he'd be much too distraught to ever consider replacing me with someone new.

For me, the only reason to bring a newcomer into the equation is if he or she truly represented a value-added.

It must also be someone a person *wants*, not someone he or she *needs*. When you *need* someone, thus begins the erasure of boundaries and tolerances. Perhaps you need someone to bring financial security and stability. Or a roof over your head. Or maybe IT expertise.

When I was much younger, there was a litany of things I felt I really needed. Accordingly, it made me susceptible to partners who were controlling. Because they perceived I was counting on them to deliver things I thought I couldn't do for myself, it gave them the leverage to essentially call all of the shots. One such relationship went so far as to tell me that if I moved in with him, all of my stuff would *obviously* have to be dispatched. Sentimentality had no place in a world in which he believed he had curated the best of the best for himself. Even my 1906 piano, he opined, was junk compared to what he could afford to replace it with if I intended to keep playing.

I remember telling Mark that if I were ever to go back and relive those relationships given what I know now, they wouldn't have been able to handle me.

"They knew they couldn't handle you *then*," he wisely replied. "Which was why they had to contain you as much as possible."

I reflect on some of the women I've met over the years whose marriages ended as a result of divorce or death. Depending on the number of years they were in a relationship, there is often a desperation to quickly find someone to fill the void, to pick up where things left off. Whether it has taken the form of hitting the bars or lonely-hearts classifieds, the salve to loneliness—and/or rejection—has been to let an empty space stay empty for as short a duration as one can.

Not only does this place unreasonable expectations on the newcomer but also engenders pressure on the part of the seeker to make everything *work*, no matter the cost. Compromising one's own values and settling for less just to have *someone, anyone* as soon as possible, however, is never a smart strategy.

And what about the men? Widowers I've known have often found themselves pounced upon by women who know how to cook and clean because these are skill sets they believe they need in order to live a comfortable existence.

"I've never seen so many casseroles and cakes and cookies in my whole life!" a friend declared in the short weeks following his wife's death. He actually snickered when I told him that becoming a widower had turned him into a primo chic magnet.

Mark would not likely have found himself in this scenario since he was already a gourmet chef and a bit of a clean-freak. He'd be a catch for certain and absolutely all of my female friends thought so even though any physical/emotional attraction to *them* was not reciprocal.

Hey, if Salma Hayek didn't have a chance, how could they?

"So what could someone do for *you*?" Mark asked me.

"I suppose they could put gas in my car," I replied.

Yes, it's true. In all the decades I had been driving, I had never once pumped my own gas.

"I should teach you how to do that," he offered.

Interestingly, the lesson didn't come until about four months before his death. In the wake of his demise, I now do this successfully all the time with both of my cars. Once either one drops to less than half a tank, I am off like a shot to the local service station, cognizant that one must always be prepared in the event of a zombie apocalypse.

I began thinking about my dear Aunt Liz. She was a very accomplished woman and a former English teacher. Yet she and Uncle Bob had a very traditional marriage in which he made the majority of their travel plans, did the gardening and pool upkeep, and paid all of the household bills. She was more than happy to go along with this arrangement.

She managed the house, did all of the cooking and Uncle Bob made killer martinis. I know the latter for a fact because I used to spend occasional weekends with them. Winter nights were always the best when the three of us—or sometimes just Aunt Liz and me—would stay up late at night in front of a crackling fireplace and solve all of the world's problems.

When Uncle Bob was hospitalized for hip replacement surgery, Aunt Liz decided to stay at a downtown hotel rather than making twice-daily trips from their beautiful home about 55 minutes away. On one such evening, she invited me to have dinner with her at the Hyatt. When the bill came, she handed it to me and asked if I would mind figuring out the tip. She confessed with great embarrassment she didn't know how to do this, that this was strictly Uncle Bob's purview and always had been.

I think I subconsciously made a note that evening this was something I should know how to do myself.

When we got married, Mark and I made the decision to keep all of our finances separate. I didn't know it at the time but this turned out to be one of the best decisions we'd ever made. I was accustomed to paying my own bills, managing my own bank account, etc., but Mark took over such things as paying the rent, handling auto and health insurance, etc. And I was more than happy to let him.

Without really realizing it, we transitioned over the course of our marriage from paper records to an online accounting platform.

In Jessica Fletcher's world, everything was probably *always* a paper platform. Come on now, this was a woman who used a manual typewriter and had a landline. Granted, she eventually segued to a laptop and a mobile, but if she had ever had to locate a paper receipt of anything she and Frank ever purchased, it would have been easy-peasy for her. From the time of my first studio apartment and bank account, I had fallen into the same category. For years, I kept copious shoeboxes of banking statements, credit card receipts and tax returns, a bit fearful of ever tossing any of them.

And yes, I was also one of those people who never tore anything off of a pillowcase or mattress. You know. Just in case.

When the hugsman was dealt the functional equivalent of a death sentence a St. Luke's, he asked me to bring his laptop to his hospital room. From there, he began the stages of shutting down his consulting business and notifying all of his clients. He also set about compiling a list of all of his passwords, his various subscriptions, automatic contract renewals and the due dates for credit card payments.

I think a lot of people are probably reticent about giving their spouses and significant others confidential info like passwords while they are still very much alive. The cynical side of me suspects they have something to hide. And yet if something unforeseen should occur, this is exactly the kind of intel their survivors will need.

Case in point: My friend whose husband had died several years previous was at a loss to even know where her spouse's checkbook was, much less know how much money was in the account.

Mark made a point of telling me that if he died before I did—and if I used his and our financial resources as wisely as he knew I would—there was enough in his life insurance policy for me to be comfortable the rest of my life. He recommended I speak with our wonderful tax guy to set up an annuity I could draw from on a monthly basis. Again, this was always a conversation which upset me for the two of us to have and yet it turned out to be a necessary one.

He also made a point of telling me who I should notify immediately if/when he passed. Social Security was an obvious one as well as the insurance agency and his 401K. Less obvious was the need to notify AAA (which had our home and auto insurance policies) and to have the public utilities switched over to my own name.

Likewise, he suggested I might want to hang onto his cell phone and maintain his email account for at least a year. The cell phone has proved invaluable on the occasions I have had to change his password in order to access his various accounts.

After I mentioned this to a friend of mine, she happened to remark that her very tech-savvy husband had set up his own cell phone to have fingerprint identification for access rather than a numeric passcode. It suddenly occurred to her that if he were to die, she'd have no way to retrieve any of his phone messages.

"If he were to be cremated or buried," she quipped, "it would be a bit awkward to ask if they could please amputate his thumb first since I might need it..."

Books and articles on widowhood contain lots of Must Do checklists. I have to admit I had never read any of them during my own crisis and was largely "winging it" for the first month.

Herein are the most important ones to pay attention to.

1. Order certified copies of death certificate. These will be supplied to you by the funeral home. They are pricey for sure but it's critical to order more than you think you will actually need. (I ordered 10.) One would think you could simply photocopy extras but there are many entities which strictly require originals. If you don't have enough and discover you need to order more, it can take anywhere from 6-10 weeks to get them.

2. Notify Social Security. If your spouse was a wage-earner (and a higher wage-earner than you), you will be entitled to his/her benefits. You cannot collect both, only the amount which is the higher. In the aftermath of COVID, many of the Social Security field offices were shut down which meant that applications could not be processed by appointment and in person. In my own experience, the Social Security website is a bit of a circuitous nightmare. Likewise, the 1-800 number which often has a wait time of at least an hour. On impulse, I dialed the nearest regional office when they opened at 8am and was surprised an actual person answered the phone.

Despite the fact the office had only a skeleton crew, this gentleman was more than happy to assist me and process my application over the phone.

3. Update information with your insurance companies and file appropriate claims. Although life insurance polices are supposed to take no longer than 30 days to process once a claim is filed, my own took a little over two months and copious phone calls.

4. Cancel your spouse's health insurance. A no-brainer, right? But easy to forget.

5. Update property titles, including vehicles. Contact the DMV to have your spouse's car title transferred to your own name.

6. Identify the executor of the estate. In our case, we were each other's executor.

7. Contact credit bureaus. These include Experian, Equifax and TransUnion. Notify any and all creditors of the death in order to freeze the accounts and ensure interest will not continue to accrue on the remaining balances. Mark and I were smart to never have comingled our finances. He was on only one credit card of mine but I requested not to be on any of his during our entire marriage. When I subsequently found out the balances on his own cards, it was a bit staggering to think of having to pay all of them off myself. Although this issue varies dramatically from state to state, I learned that the laws of the state I was living in took me off the hook insofar as being financially responsible.

8. Review debt information and acquire a financial advisor if you don't already have one.

9. Update your will and change beneficiaries. This will also include determining who will have durable power of attorney and be in charge of health care directives in the event you cannot make decisions yourself.

10. Check the contents of safes and safe deposit boxes.

11. Be patient with call center operators at credit card companies and utilities. Very often they are working from a standardized script and are not following conversations as closely as they should. Many a time I prefaced an inquiry by saying my husband had just passed away. Halfway into the chat, they would invariably ask if they could speak to him. "Only if you're doing a séance, sweetie." To which they would reply, "Huh?" The other common question I got asked was, "Would you like me to go ahead and delete him?" Hmm. Pretty sure a higher power already took care of that...

The last advice I can dispense regarding preparedness is the one thing most people don't think of until they are caught up in the swirling chaotic midst of it; specifically, how do you get the word out in a timely and respectful manner?

When I was younger, I was impressed with how newspapers could put together such lengthy and eloquent obituaries of celebrities within 24 hours of their passing. It wasn't until I worked in the media myself I discovered these write-ups and all of the requisite photographs had actually been assembled far in advance. No wonder everything seemed to flow so seamlessly!

I never revisited this topic until it came time when I knew something would have to be written and sent upon the heels of my husband's impending death.

A dear friend and colleague of his had offered to do the formal obituary for me and submit it to industry publications. Fortunately, Mark had penned so many articles and been involved in so many speaking engagements that there were numerous bios out there from which to cull the highlights of his life and professional career.

What that still left, however, was the list of friends and associates I'd need to personally contact about his passing. I decided email would be an easier route for me rather than copious phone calls. Prior to his admission to hospice care, I began putting together the list of everyone I could think of. I also began composing the body of the email I would send.

I truly had no idea how I was going to react when he actually died and whether—even as a savvy wordsmith—I'd be able to put two coherent sentences together. It was important to me not to leave anything out. I didn't tell him I was working on this but, knowing how frightfully well organized I was, I suspect he already knew and was amused by it.

And so for three nights I steadily worked on my final tribute to the man I had loved for a quarter of a century. When the call came the evening of Easter Sunday that my beloved had died peacefully in his sleep, the piece I had worked on was sent out within the first hour.

I share it here because I believe he would have wanted me to. And because it would not have been as complete and sweet and error-free if I had tried to pull all of my emotions together within the first hour of losing him.

9 April, 2023

Treasured friends and colleagues,

My apology for sending a group email. I further ask patience from those to whom I owe responses to happier emails I haven't had time in recent weeks to address. Much as I would like to write personal notes to each and every one of you, I can only ask for your quiet understanding and support as I attempt to navigate my way through the current darkness.

The love of my life—aka The Hugsman—passed quietly in his sleep this evening after a short but very fierce fight with Stage 4 cancer. It goes without saying it was a devastating shock to both of us. He was perfectly fine during the holidays but, come January, began experiencing problems with keeping food down. By the time he went to see a doctor, the disease had aggressively progressed throughout his esophagus and stomach. We were initially optimistic about radiation treatments and chemo but the sad news is that the doctors determined there was ultimately nothing they could do. Such an irony, isn't it, that two people who so loved gourmet cooking and fine wines would be hit with a fatal diagnosis which in the brief time remaining would rob my beloved of both of these.

We celebrated our 25th wedding anniversary in March. I so assumed we would be together for many, many more. A lot of you have not only known both of us individually since long before that but have also enjoyed seeing the pictures and hearing the stories of the adventures we have shared as a happily married couple with the world's cutest dog. We truly were—and still are—soulmates. We've encouraged each other in every way possible, celebrated successes, recalibrated setbacks and made all of our most important decisions at our magical dining room table. As many of you further know, he was always the first one to read new chapters in my books and do table-reads of new scripts. He assured me he'd still be doing that even after his passing; all I need do is print out the new pages and leave them face up on the table with a lovely glass of wine. I also suspect he'll be reading over my shoulder as I type. Maybe even now.

I've been asking myself time and again what I might or could have done differently to prevent this from happening. Most especially, I wish I had pushed him harder to see a doctor. His oncologist gently told me this is not a productive use of my time. In all likelihood, he said, the disease had already started years ago when he had yet to show any symptoms. I asked Mark that if he could have had a cancer-free life as a choice, would he have taken it. His response was a definitive "no." "Not if it meant I wouldn't have had you and Lucy."

When I asked him if he was afraid of dying, he squeezed my hands and softly told me he was at peace. "Going into hospice is a far better glide path and transition," he said, "than if I had been hit by a bus or was the victim of a violent crime and we hadn't been able to say goodbye." Once we knew what his fate would be, he diligently set about ensuring I'd have the resources I'd need and that I'd also know who I could turn to when he was no longer here. That's so Mark, isn't it? He even asked me to bring *his laptop to the hospital just so he could continue working as long as he possibly could.*

We are both blessed to have so many dear friends, many of whom continue to tell me how brave I am. Funny, but I don't think of myself as very brave at all. I've been pushed to the limits to do things I never thought I'd have to face...and I am enough of a realist to know this is only the tip of an iceberg, the size of which probably sank Titanic. I may be putting on a convincing brave face but on the inside I have crumbled so fast that I'm surprised I haven't just turned into a messy little pile of sawdust.

I remind myself on an almost hourly basis that in order to honor the memory of this incredible man I was privileged to call my spouse for a quarter of a century, I must soldier on and do all of the things we had talked about doing when he was still alive. Travel, of course, will be one of them. Any kindred spirits who love travel as much as we did are certainly welcome to join me. Let's make an adventure of it! My current bucket list includes Victoria British Columbia (The Empress Hotel!), Portugal, Switzerland and the Cotswolds.

I'm comforted by a quote I read from Olivia Newton John's husband. To paraphrase, he said that when one loses the love of their life, it's incumbent upon them to live as authentic and full a life as they can because they are now doing the living and adventuring for both of them. The one who has left will always be there in spirit and will, thus, be happy to see their survivor tapping every last drop of their own existence until such time as they are reunited in the afterlife.

Mark, by the by, has already promised to haunt me...but in a good way. Hopefully it won't be in a weird way like Alan Rickman as Jamie in "Truly, Madly, Deeply" in which he'll be rearranging the furniture, fussing with the thermostat and inviting his mates in to watch old movies while I'm in the bathtub. The first time I watched that film, I always thought Jamie had come back because he was so lonely and wasn't adjusting to his new status. I have now gleaned a new appreciation that he came back because he wanted his beloved to be able to move on with her own life. If you've never seen it or haven't seen it in a while, I recommend giving it a watch and understanding what I'm saying.

I've already had many friends, colleagues and even total strangers asking if there is anything they can do. Mark told me I must absolutely take each person up on his/her offer rather than trying to do everything myself as the theatre director in me is normally wont to do. Maybe it will be something big (i.e., How do I order spare parts for a Harrier jump jet); Maybe it will be something small like teaching me how to make an espresso or set up a Zoom account; It might even be something seemingly stupid (to you) (i.e., what jobs in Egyptian times still exist today) but that would help me research something obscure for a new book or play.

I also want to be surprised by spontaneous flowers and I don't want any of you to fess up to being the sender(s). I know there will be an outpouring of lovely blooms in the coming weeks but what about summer or the holidays or five years from now? One of the things I always loved about Mark was his spontaneity. He'd come home with a bouquet and when I asked the occasion, he'd say, "Because it's Tuesday and I love you." And so whenever you hear him whisper in your ear, "I think Christina needs a rose today," just send it and sign the card with love from Mark. I won't know it's from you but Mark will and it will gladden his heart to have such comforting friends around me long after he had left us.

For the time being, Lucy and I plan to stay at Dobbs Mill. Mark and I had deemed this our forever home when we moved here two years ago, never anticipating that only one of us would still be alive on that anniversary. Come December, I may not have the emotional bandwidth to do our usual festive Christmas cards. (Although I do suspect that for all of these years I could have just sent a card with a collage of Lucy images and everyone would have been fine with that.)

Mark's absence has been especially hard on her. It tears my heart out when we come back from a walk and she either races into Mark's office or wants to go into the garage. She sees his car there and she just knows he has to be around somewhere. Although she has always slept with us, she has now taken to sleeping on his pillow and being a comfort to me. At 13 years old, she still looks and acts like a puppy and I hope to have her around for as long as she continues to be healthy and happy.

We only have each other now and we shall make the most of every moment, especially with long walks around the lake and appreciating the beauty of nature. Thankfully I was able to take her to visit him in the private home offering hospice. I'm not sure who was the happier to see whom. She immediately jumped up on the bed to give him sweet kisses, then hopped off to go investigate the rest of the house. I think it had her approval.

As I write, I am listening to the opening theme music from one of my favorite television shows from the 90s. (https://www.youtube.com/watch?v=Kp6C5dH-_OQ). Not only was "Wings" great casting and writing but I always found an optimism to it with the idea behind freedom of flight, open skies and pursuit of dreams. I must also admit I enjoyed the romantic ambiance of the quaint Nantucket setting itself. Maybe I'll add that one to my travel list as well.

It's not the first time I have been alone. I was alone for quite a few years before Mark ever swept me off my feet and proposed to me on our first date. Once that happened, I'd never have thought I'd one day be alone again and have to relearn how to be self-sufficient. How will I be as a new widow, I wonder. One thing for certain is that I won't succumb to being a recluse (there are just too many of you who won't let me) or viewed by the neighbors as that crazy lady who talks to ducks as much as she talks to herself.

I told Mark my role model would likely be Jessica Fletcher (Angela Lansbury) from Murder, She Wrote. I'll enjoy a close-knit community, write wonderful mysteries, help the police solve crimes and even occasionally be wined and dined by dashing older men whom I will subsequently have to turn in for murder before dessert even arrives. I will continue to practice the piano, practice Portuguese, take my vitamins and even return to cooking gourmet meals for myself and friends.

It will by no means be easy. I take solace in the fact my beloved is no longer in pain and that we'll one day be reunited. He promises to scope out the Hereafter and learn the ropes so he can show me around. I told him I'd join him as soon as I could and he replied, "Please don't, my love. Take all of the time you want and need in the Here and Now. You'll just have that many more stories to tell me when we catch up."

As I close, I invite you to play the theme music once again, picture Mark confidently taking off on a beautiful day, enjoying a magnificent bird's eye view of a place he so loved and then touching down safely and comfortably, Home at last.

Remember him fondly and feel the same gratitude I feel that we were oh so lucky to know him.

Even forever would not have been long enough.

In the weeks that followed, a number of friends complimented me on what I had written and expressed surprise I could have composed something so articulate under such stress. Several of them later asked if I could write up something which their *own* relatives might use when the time comes.

Who knows? I may have found a new specialty niche for my wordsmithing: Obits R Us.

CREMATION GUY
AND THE GREAT
HALL OF URNS

I belong to a number of writers groups on Facebook and one of the most common questions I see newbies posting is whether established authors ever draw inspiration for their characters from real-life people they actually know.

Happens way more often than people think. Golly, but some of us even use similar names, attributes and physical descriptions which would make the fictional personae instantly recognizable to one's inner circle.

Years ago when I was writing romantic suspense for HarperCollins, I crafted a nosey and dislikeable housekeeper after a particularly nosey and dislikeable supervisor in the division where I worked. Two of my best friends—Jon and Kevin—were excited to read the book because I had promised both of them good roles in it. No sooner had they finished when they separately came to me and said, "So is the bossy housekeeper Gwen?"

Such discerning lads that they not only recognized her straightaway as my office nemesis but were also more than delighted when she got impaled under the iron portcullis on a dark and stormy night.

I've often wondered if Jessica Fletcher's murder mysteries were replete with the various villains she encountered in Cabot Cove and, later, New York. Likewise, did she favorably pepper her plots with the friends and helpmates who rounded out her life at 698 Candlewood Lane? Certainly the local sheriffs—Mort Metzger and Amos Tupper—would have had as prestigious slots as the town doc (Seth Hazlitt), JB's nephew (Grady), or occasional visitor and private eye Harry McGraw (played by the amazing Jerry Orbach).

One need look no farther than the show's creator to suspect this wordsmithing practice is true. Following his retirement from Tinseltown, my prolific friend Peter launched his successful *Hollywood Murder Mysteries* series in which real-life celebrities interacted with workaday folks such as his protagonist sleuth, Joe Bernardi. It was a no-brainer that the unmasked killer(s) would never be someone who had been a famous fixture in film and television since history could clearly not be rewritten just to satisfy a plot twist.

But what about everyone else? Peter confided he often "cast" friends and enemies as, respectively, good guys and bad guys. In one of his books, for instance, savvy readers will even spot two minor characters with the names "Mark" and "Christina."

Obviously I was doing this long before Peter and I became friends. Woe to bad bosses, ex-boyfriends, crazy relatives, etc.—all of whom continue to make appearances as characters my readers love to hate. Some, in fact, even have the distinction of becoming chalk outlines on the floor. Little wonder that someone came up with a tee-shirt which says, "Careful or you'll end up in my next novel."

All of which leads to the next completely weird—but absolutely true—story of honoring Mark's wishes for cremation.

This particular tale points up the need to discuss your loved one's wishes for cremation or burial long *before* you actually have to make such decisions. I'm sure there are plenty of lovely people who have made the mortuary business their professional calling. It saddens be, however, that there are those who know how to prey on the vulnerability, grief and confusion which sets in immediately following a death. (Think of Liberace as Mr. Starker, the Whispering Glades Casket Salesman, in Tony Richardson's *The Loved One*.)

When you're not in your right mind, it would be easy enough for someone to guilt you into buying something you can't afford and, further, that your beloved might not even have wanted.

During a break in which the nurses had come in to chat with him (I do think he was one of their most charming and engaged patients), I borrowed Mark's laptop to see what I could suss out about cremation services.

My task was instantly rewarded with direction to a website which offered an all-inclusive price of $995. Never having researched this before, I had no idea whether this was a smart deal or not. I was only familiar with what friends had told me about the exorbitant price of coffins which their relatives had purchased for themselves or vested family members to purchase *for* them. Clearly many of the older ones had wanted nothing but the Best of the Best for their final resting receptacle, a testament to the notion of going out in grand style.

Much of this, I think, was to show well for the funeral services prior to being covered with six feet of dirt and never being seen again. Not only were these constructed from extremely expensive and highly polished woods but the interiors absolutely had to have plush velvet and satin, Memory Foam, and Surround-Sound.

Seriously.

I'm not sure how the deceased is supposed to appreciate these pricey amenities but each to their own.

I decided to give the business a call, introduce myself and find out what, exactly, I'd be getting for my $995. Surreal, yes, to be conducting this conversation while Mark was very much still alive in his hospital bed just across the room but he, too, was curious about how this whole thing worked.

The funeral director advised me that the cost would cover the pick-up of the deceased, the actual cremation and provision of the ashes themselves.

"And, of course, you'll be wanting to purchase an urn from us," he informed me.

"Actually," I replied, "we've already talked about it and have our own plan."

"*Oh?*"

Was it just me or had the temperature dropped perceptibly in his tone?

Prior to my conversation with the man who would hereinafter be referred to as Cremation Guy, I had asked Mark what he wanted me to do with his ashes. He most definitely did not want to be interred at a cemetery which would have required me to go visit him. In this regard, I'm sure he was channeling some of his own guilt at never having gone to visit his father. With the exception of the military honor guard who performed the ceremony, Mark and I had been the only two people in attendance, his dad not really having a cadre of pals at the time of his death.

Nor did we have a garden which, at some point, might have required Mark's urn to be dug up if there was a change in ownership.

"Just keep me someplace close to you," he requested.

And that's when I hit upon the perfect idea and in keeping with our respectively wacky senses of humor.

Years ago we had enjoyed a wonderful lunch at Il Fornaio in Old Town Pasadena and ordered an expensive bottle of French champagne (Beau Joie Brut Rose, to be specific). The bottle itself was encased in elegantly burnished metal latticework which gave it the look and heft of something Indiana Jones would go questing after to protect from Nazis. After the meal, I asked if we could keep the bottle.

"You paid for it," our server quipped. "By all means."

We brought it home and put it on a small table in the dining room as a prop for our metal winged dragon, Diavlo.

"So here's what I'm thinking," I said to Mark in the hospital. "How would you like to be decanted into the champagne bottle and guarded by Diavlo?"

Mark thought this was very funny but pointed out that, being a big guy, he didn't really think all of his ashes would fit.

I, of course, already had an answer to that as well. I told him I'd decant as much of him as *would* fit and that I'd save the rest for future travels so he could be scattered hither and thither across the country and around the world.

"So here's our plan," I cheerfully told Cremation Guy. "I'd like you to put my husband's ashes in a champagne bottle."

Stony silence, followed by, "We can't do that."

I reminded him that the wording on the website was quite clear about wanting to honor the wishes of the deceased and the deceased's family. "We've talked this over and this is what we both want."

"*Most* people," he sternly emphasized, "would want something more tasteful and respectful."

"Yes, maybe so. But the bottle is really quite elegant."

Not like I was sticking him in a cheap bottle of Gallo *Boone's Farm* fruitiness, right?

I started to relate what fond memories it conjured of the great lunch we had but he sharply cut me off with the advisement that my request went against company policy and could not be encouraged.

Heavens but did he think I was trying to set a precedent in which—once the word got out—*everyone* would want to be put into champagne bottles?

My assumption was that maybe he didn't want to risk dropping the bottle on the floor and breaking it. I even offered to sign a waiver if something untoward happened during the decanting.

This guy became an immovable object. "*Most* people," he insisted, "want only the *best* for their loved ones."

"Trust me," I replied, "I am sooooo not 'most people'. Now can we work something out here?"

Oblivious to my request, he proceeded to tell me what a fine selection of urns he sold on the premises and that he was certain he could assist me in finding something appropriate.

"Oh, I'm sure you could," I said, "but that's not what the two of us want."

Across the room, Mark was smiling. From the half of the conversation he was hearing, he later told me it was taking on all the hilarity of a *Seinfeld* episode.

I very respectfully asked Cremation Guy why I had to buy an urn from him at all.

He matter of factly informed me that ashes could absolutely *not* be interred in anything which was brought in from the outside.

Sounds a bit like movie theatres which discourage patrons from sneaking in their own sodas and Milk Duds.

I asked Cremation Guy what my husband's ashes would be put in if I *didn't* purchase an urn.

He tersely replied that they had standard black plastic boxes containing baggies with twisty-ties. This, it turned out, was included in the $995 special. Also included would be Mark's full name and date of death, courtesy of a nifty Dymo label-maker.

Hey, because Heaven forbid I should run across the box someday in the attic and say, "What the heck is in *here*?"

I was unabashed in my observation that the box, baggie and twisty tie sounded a smidge tacky.

"*That*, Madam, is why *most* people—"

"You know if you start one more flippin' sentence with the phrase 'most people,' I may need to reconsider all of this." In the next breath, I asked if there was anything illegal about my bringing the crappy black box home and decanting the ashes myself at our center kitchen island.

Even over the phone, I could tell he was ruffled I'd even propose something so unseemly. Good thing I never mentioned anything about Diavlo or I'm pretty sure he'd be convinced I was some sort of a witch.

"I mean, how hard can it be?" I blithely continued. "A plastic funnel, a little scooper..."

He interrupted to emphasize the sacrilege of accidentally spilling any of the ashes during the process.

"Oh, no worries," I replied. "I'll put down a placemat first."

When Mark was moved into hospice care, I let his caregivers know I had already spoken with Cremation Guy and gave them the number to call. They were impressed, I think, that I had sussed all of this out in advance. Apparently, caregivers are often left to make such arrangements themselves and have various funeral homes on speed-dial.

Mark's body was picked up the evening of Easter Sunday. First thing Monday morning Cremation Guy called to tell me (in what I felt was an inappropriately cheery voice) that he had made the pick-up.

"Would you care to come for a viewing?" he inquired.

"Thank you but I so would not."

I'm sure he was biting the tip of his tongue to keep from saying this was something most people liked to do.

He went on to suggest I might like to come out to be apprised of the actual process which would take place.

Again, a solid no. Pretty sure I could just use my imagination for this.

Cremation Guy informed me I'd have to come to the facility anyway to sign the documents authorizing the cremation. I requested the documents be emailed to me.

He balked at this and told me my signature wouldn't be legally binding.

"Actually," I replied, "electronic signatures are legal in all fifty states and even a lot of foreign countries."

He grudgingly consented to do this. "And, of course," he added, "we require full payment upfront."

Interestingly, he had no problem whatsoever sending me the *bill* electronically. In less than a minute of my putting the $995 on a credit card, he immediately processed it and emailed me a receipt.

The next question I put to him was approximately how long things would take.

"Well, your husband *did* die on a holiday weekend." Was there a censorious undertone to this statement to suggest Mark had planned his Easter Sunday exit on purpose just to mess with their schedule? "We have a backlog."

"Okaaaaay. So how long before the backlog might become unjammed?"

He wasn't sure of this but responded that Mark would be put in the queue.

In the queue.

Strange phraseology, isn't it, to use for cremation services? My imagination conjured a macabre ride at an amusement park in which a line-up of cardboard coffins moves on a conveyor belt operated by a pert miss at a podium who systematically controls when each coffin will cross the threshold and be sent over the fiery brink.

Cremation Guy intruded on my musings to say he'd let me know when my husband had been cremated. "And perhaps," he added, "it will give you more time to think about the purchase of an appropriate urn."

Talk about determination not to give up and miss out on a sale.

He called me two days later—Wednesday by now—with the cheery news that Mark's ashes were available to be picked up.

My next question was whether the ashes could be delivered to me at home.

His voice went up a few decibels. "We don't *do* deliveries!"

Curious that they could do pick-ups of a full-grown male corpse and yet couldn't swing by the same neighborhood and drop off a crappy black plastic box.

I told him I'd get back to him.

"Well, don't take longer than 30 days," he warned me. "We don't have the space to store ashes *forever*, you know."

My husband's best friend, Saul, had asked me if there was anything he could do. Although I was perfectly capable of driving to the mortuary to collect Mark's ashes myself, the real puzzler was where I was going to put the box in my Mazda Miata. If I put it in the trunk and took a sharp turn, would all of the ashes fall out? Could I strap the box into the passenger seat? The third alternative was to put the box between my legs as I drove.

Which Mark would probably have enjoyed.

Saul offered to fly up from Los Angeles and asked if we could arrange the pick-up on a Saturday.

Cremation Guy informd me that Saturday pick-ups were not allowed. Seriously. I have no idea who makes up these silly rules.

A Friday would have meant Saul would have to take the day off from work. Which, of course, he was happy to do. In return, I'd fix him dinner Friday night, we could decant Mark's ashes together and he could fly home on Saturday.

The first Friday that Cremation Guy had available was April 21st. Coincidentally, my birthday.

"I have three time slots available," he said. "11:30, 12:45 and 2:25."

"You mean you don't have something like a theatre Will Call window where I can just pick them up when we get there?"

If I hadn't figured it out before, Cremation Guy was completely lacking in any sense of humor. He repeated the three available times, intent on running as tight a ship as possible.

I chose 2:25 just in case there were any possible hiccups with Southwest Airlines.

At this point, I think Saul was as curious as I was about what Cremation Guy physically looked like. Saul's bet was on Lurch from *The Addams Family*. I was picturing an older Lenny from *Laverne and Shirley*. (My own guess was closer, although neither one of us expected that Cremation Guy's complexion didn't seem to have any pores. Weird, right?)

When we arrived, I was presented with a plethora of paperwork and asked to produce two pieces of identification to prove who I was. (Are there really that many strangers who run around to mortuaries and collect ashes of people they don't even know?)

At long last I was presented with The Box and its twisty tie baggy of cremains. He made a point of showing me the label as reassurance I wasn't taking a total stranger home by mistake.

Cremation Guy somberly invited us to sit for as long as we wanted in the adjacent Serenity Room. While I was signing the final paperwork, Saul ventured a peek and mouthed "Great Hall of Urns." Yes, I do believe Cremation Guy was going to make one last ditch effort to make a sale.

Perhaps if Saul and I had physically crossed the threshold, the doors would have immediately been bolted behind us and it would have become like a freaky timeshare presentation in which we wouldn't be let out until my checkbook was five figures lighter.

Suffice it to say, we beat a hasty but polite retreat. That evening the two of us gave Mark the send-off he would have wanted with a plastic funnel, a scoop and a placemat.

I have never seen Diavlo look happier than to have his own "hooman" to guard for all eternity.

A month or so later, I was invited by Chaplain Charly at the hospice organization to avail myself of the grief counseling services it provided. "It sounds like you're doing really well," he complimented me, "but you may pick up a few tips to help down the road."

I think the fact I shared the Cremation Guy story with him during that phone call was all the assurance he needed that my sense of humor was going to see me through.

The group met once a week for six weeks with a nice lunch provided. Such a calming, nurturing environment for the participants to talk about their loved ones and reach for the Kleenex boxes as often as they needed to.

Near the end of the first session, Charly remarked that we still had ten minutes left and did anyone want to add anything. When no more stories were forthcoming, he turned to me and said, "So, Christina? Maybe you could share the story of Cremation Guy..."

I so did not see *that* coming, especially with a group of mourners I had never met. Would they be aghast and find my tale as shocking and disrespectful as Cremation Guy himself? Charly, however, was nodding and smiling encouragement and I realized he probably knew this audience better than I did.

By the time I finished, the members of the group were laughing in spite of themselves. And this, I think, was the wisdom of his invitation—to remind them that—even in the midst of tragedy—laughter can lighten our souls and remind us of its healing capabilities.

As I was walking out to the parking lot, one of the elderly new widows in the group rushed to catch up with me. "I so enjoyed your funny story about that horrid Cremation Man," she said.

She then proceeded to tell me that her late husband, Ernie, had loved fine wines but that he had hated to throw out the bottles when they were finished because the labels were so pretty. Down in the basement, she continued, she had all of these beautiful bottles she didn't know what to do with and did I think maybe she should do the same thing I did with the champagne bottle.

On the one hand, I was flattered to be such a quirky influencer. On the other hand, it struck me as a smidge sad that this was a woman whose husband of 50+ years had probably made all of the major decisions in their life together. For the first time, she was now having to make decisions herself and was seeking out a total stranger for advice.

I told her that, like Mark, her beloved likely wouldn't fit within the confines of a single bottle and she might need to use a couple of them. She thought this was a good idea and merrily went on her way.

At the next group meeting, she got there early and saved me a place right next to her. "I took your advice," she said, positively beaming. It had apparently taken half a dozen bottles of "decanting" but she now had a smart little row of Ernies marching across the fireplace mantle.

And she had me to thank for it.

THE GOOD STUFF

Did you ever see Jessica Fletcher eat off a paper plate, tuck into Chinese food straight out of the carton or microwave a Lean Cuisine for her dinner? If she drank tea or coffee as she worked, it was likely out of a large ceramic mug gifted to her by her former students, never a Styrofoam cup. Whether she was entertaining or dining alone, the meal was probably served on the Staffordshire Liberty Blue plates which graced her Victorian breakfront.

After all, who better to spoil herself and dine in style than the Queen of Amateur Sleuths?

Of the many silly questions I was asked after Mark's passing was the one about what I was now going to do with all of our plates, placemats, stemware, napkins and napkin rings. The *Culinary Capers* in which we indulged friends on Facebook every Monday evening left no doubt we had acquired a sizable collection of all of these things.

While we both knew people who were perfectly content eating off the same plates every single day, our own philosophy was that different cuisine called for different tablescaping. Would you, for instance, hang every picture you owned in exactly the same color and style of frame? Whether it was Mexican, Chinese, French, Indonesian, Moroccan, etc., we had the patterns, colors and sizes to show each dish off to its best advantage. On the occasions we hosted small dinner parties, the first thing our guests always noticed was the dining room table and how it had been artfully staged as a teaser for the evening to come.

"But it's not like you'll actually be *using* any of it now..."

Hmm. Did they expect the sight of all that tableware we had acquired during our marriage would plunge me into such a state of depression as to swear off eating entirely? I must have missed that memo.

I replied that I still intended to have guests over since I especially enjoy cooking. It's one of the reasons, in fact, we have never had a guest bedroom. I do believe it would take only meal for them to never want to leave.

"Yes, but it's not like you'll be using any of it when you're just by *yourself...*"

To the contrary. Even if I am only eating a sandwich and some crisps for lunch, there's no reason it won't be on Art Deco china and with a linen napkin in my lap. A cocktail in the evening is often in a crystal martini glass. And why *not* make an event of breakfast at the dining room table instead of scarfing down a piece of toast while standing at the center island?

For all of our years together, Mark and I made a point of making an occasion out of even the simplest routines. We'd both had grandparents—and even parents—who kept "the good stuff" under lock and key, bringing it out only for holiday dinners. How sad that all of those beautiful plates and goblets and lace tablecloths spent ninety percent of their existence out of anyone's sight. The excuse was that these items were only for "special" occasions. Goodness, but what's more special than celebrating day-to-day joys and accomplishments?

Obviously it makes a difference if one constantly has children underfoot and everything has to be kept out of reach for its own safety. At the same time, I've known plenty of parentals who have impressed upon their offspring that "Do Not Touch" means exactly that. A healthy respect for breakables at a young age should hopefully manifest into an appreciation for these same items when they are older.

Assuming that your own children are grown by now and that you don't see your grandchildren on a daily basis, there's no excuse not to indulge yourself as a new widow and bring out every treasure whose memories make you smile. Instead of hiding them away, bring them out and celebrate the tales behind how they came into your life to begin with.

Were you just starting your journey together? Was this a significant anniversary? Was it handed down by a family ancestor? Were you traveling and saw something in a window that you just couldn't go home without?

Almost everything has a story and those stories are meant to be shared in order to keep their existence vibrant...and blissfully sentimental.

Do you have rooms in your house which you feel compelled to leave exactly as they were when your spouse was still alive? If you happen to like them exactly as they are, there's certainly no reason to change things up.

For me, three rooms come to mind which could be ripe for redecoration.

The first is the master bedroom. Depending on your finances, it may not be practical at the outset to invest in brand new furniture or paint all of the walls a different hue. At a minimum, though, you could spring for new sheets, a new comforter and new throw pillows. And don't buy cheap crap, either. You know the luxuriating feeling you get when you stay in a hotel room or B&B and everything just invites you to want to sleep in and slumber all day? The good stuff in which they have invested for your comfort is to entice you to come back. Shouldn't your bedroom invoke the same comforting sensations?

Secondly is the master bathroom. Assuming the two of you shared this space, it probably represents a compromise of masculine and feminine tastes. Well, sweetie, it is now completely yours. Empty the drawers which were his and fill them with every fun eye shadow and lip gloss you ever wanted to try along with all the free samples that department stores give out with fragrance purchases. If you always wanted an Edwardian shower curtain, tiered metal and glass trays for your perfumes and cosmetics, and a plush Turkish rug to tickle your toes when you get out of your bubble bath, there is nothing stopping you. Just make it good stuff which will bring longevity to the equation.

The third room depends on whether your spouse had a separate home office. The downstairs bedroom which Mark used for his consulting business also serves as my music room (since there was no way I was going to trust the movers to take my 1906 upright grand up a flight of stairs). I was happy enough with his corner desk and all of the bookcases but within the first eight months I began transforming it into a space I'd be happy to use as a second office for myself. Not only was a lot of the art repurposed for other rooms but I additionally refinished a 1950s Danish Modern buffet ("good stuff" by the standards of modern furniture-making), added a vintage lamp and purchased a one-of-a-kind Asian cabinet in teal which now houses all of my sheet music.

The Asian cabinet is a special story in itself. We first saw it at a home décor business when we moved to Dobbs Mill in 2021. Although we both fell in love with it, Mark pointed out that we didn't have any place to put it. (I, of course, liken it to his ongoing challenge of telling me we didn't have enough wall space for any more Charles Wysocki lithographs.)

Fast forward to the end of 2023. I had frequent occasion to visit the shop since it was in the same plaza as my nail salon. I confessed confusion to the store's designer that this magnificent cabinet had yet to be sold after all this time. Because of the unique color and style, she explained, it was just different and eclectic enough to make it a difficult match for most people's existing decor. "Which is sad," she added, "because this is really good stuff." Ah yes, the operative phrase.

The week before Christmas, I told myself that if it was still on the floor by the first week of January, it was a sign I was supposed to have it.

And I do. And it's perfect.

The "good stuff" label also goes for items of apparel which make you feel good about yourself. I recall an older friend who kept several dresser drawers of silky lingerie. Whether or not they had been purchased for a romantic special occasion, her relatives were astonished by their discovery, especially since many of them still had tags on them. What was she saving them for? She did the same with her jewelry—squillions of cute bracelets, brooches, pendants. A sparkle a day around her wrist, neck or fingers might have made her smile, even if she never left the house.

When Mark died, I did an overhaul of my lingerie drawer. Although my inventory was lovely to begin with, I decided I needed more lace, more silk, more satin, more colors. Even though at the time I wasn't sure if anyone would ever see these sexy purchases besides myself, it didn't stop me from buying them Just Because.

Perhaps that same mindset can prevail with you. Slip on that saucy lace thong with the matching bra. Model them in front of the mirror. Put your clothes on over them and go out and seize the day. No one will have any clue what's really under your jeans and sweatshirt but that's not the point. *You'll* know. And it will put a confident spring in your step that every new widow deserves to experience.

Need more self-care ideas? Try these:

Make the fudge. Lick the bowl.

Put on your favorite song. Sing along with it and play it 47 times.

Read a new novel while you eat dinner.

Indulge in your favorite tea. Buy a china cup and saucer for it.

Buy a cookie. Buy two. Don't share it.

Stay in your jammies on a rainy day. All day.

Watch and re-watch your favorite movies.

Browse in a bookstore.

Sing in a shower. (The acoustics are amazing!)

Start a gratitude journal and commit to writing in it every day.

Give yourself a facial.

Make a date once a week with a friend for coffee, lunch or wine.

Dance in the kitchen in your socks.

Get a haircut or highlight. Splurge on a mani and pedi.

Make a list of 10 things you want to do which require neither the permission nor the approval of anyone else.

Treat yourself to a picnic even if it is indoors.

Celebrate your half-birthday.

Learn a new language.

Soak in a bubble bath.

Volunteer for a cause you believe in.

Get your jam on in the grocery store when your favorite song comes on. Don't fret about looking silly. Everyone else probably wants to do it, too. You can encourage them in this by doing it first.

Make hot chocolate and don't skimp on the frothy whipped cream.

Be kind to total strangers.

Drink lemonade or soda out of a stemmed glass.

Spend time in sadness. Just don't make it your permanent address.

Binge-watch your favorite television series.

Create a Zen garden.

Close your eyes, imagine your happiest place and fall asleep re-living the best of times.

Comb travel brochures. Plan virtual solo vacations in advance of going on your next real one.

Take long walks and skaddle through dry leaves.

Meditate at least 15 minutes a day.

Join a book club, whether online or in person.

Compile a playlist of your favorite songs.

Take a class in something you've always wanted to know more about.

Treat yourself to breakfast in bed on a lovely tray.

Learn to say "no".

Put on your Wellies and go splash in puddles.

Invite your best gal pals for a slumber party. Add wine.

Buy a bubble maker and run outside with it.

Get a humidifier and some essential oils for a dreamy night's sleep.

Drink a full glass of water first thing every morning.

Buy yourself fresh flowers.

Practice deep breathing.

Get on the floor and play with your dog or cat.

Throw your sheets in the dryer right before bedtime so you can fall asleep in cozy warmth.

Eat your favorite breakfast for dinner.

Get up early to watch the sunrise.

Go to bed late and stand under the moon and stars.

It's all good stuff. And it's nothing less than you should enjoy.

Just Because.

HAPPY HAUNTINGS
AND FACING
FORWARD IN THE
NOW

While Mark was in St. Luke's, we had opportunity for some philosophical discussions about his next journey. For what else could we call it *but* a journey when it involved moving from a physical plane to an ethereal one?

Mark was not a practicing Catholic. In fact he had only become one during his first marriage when his ex-wife insisted he'd probably go to Hell if he didn't convert. Now and again on his lunch hour he'd pop into a downtown cathedral for contemplation but—unlike one of my exes—never expected me to accompany him or blocked off Sunday mornings for regular worship.

His complete calmness in the face of death is something I will always admire. He also expressed relief he wasn't going to linger for months on end. The frustration of not being able to do things for himself was matched only by his fear of the stress it would exact on me as his system began shutting down.

We speculated whether there was a large ARRIVALS board in Heaven such as those found in airports and whether our already departed friends check this every morning to see if there is someone they know.

My former boss, Thatcher, had a particularly booming voice and I can easily hear him announcing, "Hey, everybody! Mark's flight just got in!"

And there would be a happy crowd to greet him, show him the ropes, introduce him to the choirmaster, and direct him to the midnight buffet where he could make smart commentary on the food and wine.

I had made a point of not mentioning Mark's illness to Peter, primarily because I didn't want to upset him. Peter, however, was deep in his 80s by now. "You do know I'll probably run into him one day soon," Mark remarked, "and he'll be confused why you didn't tell him." (Peter himself passed away in October of 2023.)

Knowing Peter, he'd more likely declare, "Mark! What the Hell are *you* doing here?" And then they'd laugh and Peter would take him off to see Lucille, Jerry Orbach and Angela Lansbury.

"I do envy you all of the cool people you'll get to meet," I told Mark.

He asked if I had a list of individuals he should seek out on my behalf.

Definitely Jerry Orbach and Angela Lansbury. "And Queen Elizabeth and her mum." I'd always thought we'd get along famously, especially given our mutual love of dogs and horses.

I also said he should make a point of seeking out Alan Rickman and letting him know I do an absolute killer impression of him. (It's all in the nose, the lip sneer and the pacing.)

And just think about the cool chefs with whom he could commiserate: Julia Child, Paul Prudhomme, Elizabeth Lambert Ortiz, James Beard. He had all of their cookbooks and would love to pick their brains and learn more about their respective approaches to cooking.

On a more serious note, he promised to look after Lucy and me.

"You mean as in haunting us?"

"Yes. But only in a good way."

He had long been apprised of my belief that if someone consistently wakes up at three in the morning, it's because someone from the other side is trying to communicate. Mark interpreted this as an open channel and said he'd remember this accessibility once he settled into his new after-life. He expressed the hope I'd continue to talk to him and ask his advice. He had no idea whether I'd be able to hear any of his responses but that he would endeavor to find a way to let me know he was still around.

For me, one of the biggest losses was his skill as a proofreader and editor. As I was working on my UK cozy mystery series, I'd print out fresh chapters for him to read over adult beverages at the dining room table. This actually turned out to be great incentive for me to write as quickly as I could. Heaven forbid that he would come to the cocktail hour and there wasn't any new content for him to review!

During the first three months after his death, I continued the practice of setting out new chapters at his place along with a pen. Just in case. I'd check each morning but the pen hadn't moved, nor were there any mark-ups on my pages.

Apparently the learning curve in the Hereafter is a slow one. I was whimsically reminded of the role Patrick Swayze played in the 1990 supernatural film, *Ghost*. Murdered by a business colleague and close friend, Patrick's ghost is forced to swan about powerlessly as he watches his beloved Molly get drawn into dangerous circumstances which threaten her own existence.

How totally frustrating to discover you're a ghost but that you can't freely walk through walls, levitate furniture or, most importantly, let your voice be heard from beyond the veil. When the movie's newbie ghost enlists the aid of a poltergeist on the New York subway to teach him the basics about moving objects, I can't help but wonder if the hugsman isn't seeking out kindred spirits in the writing profession who can show him how to turn pages and pick up a pen.

To my knowledge, there were only three episodes of *Murder, She Wrote* in which Jessica Fletcher was consulted regarding the influence of supernatural forces. In all three—"Reflections of the Mind," "Nan's Ghost" and "Angel of Death"—she pragmatically reviewed the facts and took little time in determining that very human villains were using the susceptibility/gullibility of their targets to scheme and connive.

Though nothing was ever alluded to in the series that Jessica's late husband, Frank, paid her any visits, I'm sure she'd employ that same level of logic and pragmatism, listen thoughtfully to whatever he had to say and then tell him she really had to get back to work because she was on deadline with her publisher.

On the subject of ghosts, theatre lovers may recall that Angela Lansbury played the ditzy Madame Arcati in *Blithe Spirit* on Broadway, a role for which she won another of her Tony awards. Like the character of Oda Mae Brown (played by Whoopi Goldberg) in *Ghost*, Madame Arcati is as surprised as anyone else by her own talents as a clairvoyant and unsettled by what those talents can unwittingly release.

So why *do* ghosts engage in haunting the living?

Experts on the subject claim that it usually has to do with unfinished business on Earth. Victims of crimes obviously want their deaths avenged and their killers punished. Those who were happy and in love just want the best for the ones they left behind and perhaps believe they can ensure that by maintaining an otherworldly presence.

Thus far, the hugsman's hauntings have manifested in the form of playing with the lights on the fairy tree in the dining room, futzing with the thermostat and moving the Turkish rug in my home office.

The lights I can understand. Friends have explained that spirits are fascinated by illumination and electricity.

The thermostat is a no-brainer as well. Many a time when we'd be sitting in the living room, Mark would ask if I thought the room was too cold. "I don't know. Maybe," I'd reply. Up he'd leap to make an adjustment. About twenty minutes later he'd ask if the room was too warm. If I answered in the affirmative, up he'd leap again to futz with the settings. Nowadays I find that no matter what temperature I set, it will have changed of its own accord a few minutes later.

The real puzzler is the Turkish rug. After his death, I bought a new one for the master bedroom. Multiple times throughout the day, it managed to move from its original placement. I knew it wasn't Lucy because she only weighs ten pounds. Nor was it in a high traffic pattern where I could have been sliding it about myself.

I finally determined that maybe he just didn't like it. I bought a different rug and moved the first one into my office. The result is that the replacement rug has stayed put. The one in my office, however, continues to move a few inches east/west every day despite one side of it being anchored by a heavy black stove.

I have no idea what this means, nor does it make sense that if he can move a 5x8 foot rug, he can't wield a much, much lighter pen and actually make himself useful.

Interestingly, the day I was rolling up the first rug and replacing it with the second one, there was a bright green praying mantis on the screen outside the master bedroom window. He was cocking his little triangular head quizzically and, sensitive to the mythology surrounding these creatures, I proceeded to have a one-sided conversation with him about what I was doing and why I was doing it. The mantis name, after all, derives from the Greek word for "seer" or "prophet". Maybe he knew something I didn't? They have long been associated with mindfulness and the message to slow down and tap into stillness.

By the time I had successfully made the rug swap, my little green friend had flown away.

I am a firm believer in genuine psychics (operative word *genuine*) and am fortunate to have two in my life whose counsel I implicitly trust. The reason for this trust is that they have told me hilariously obscure things known only to Mark and me and, further, they have never asked for any money for the extraordinary gifts they possess.

There are certainly charlatans aplenty who prey on the vulnerability of those who have lost a loved one, and it saddens me that in the quest to seek answers/forgiveness/permission they would part with large sums of cash to complete strangers who promise savvy solace.

In an earlier era, one needed only to troll the obituaries, attend funerals and ask the right questions of townsfolk in order to put together a victim profile on which to build some plausible soothsaying. In the age of technology, this job has been made even easier by those who use social media as a daily diary of their hopes, fears, regrets and what they ate for dinner last Thursday.

I do cringe a bit whenever I see widows and widowers post intimate details on Facebook about their loved ones and the tremendous sorrow they are enduring. Accordingly, I'd be doing a disservice to readers of this book if I didn't encourage discretion in oversharing on platforms which, frankly, anyone can read and take advantage of. If you *do* decide to seek advice from mediums, my three recommendations are to do readings in person, pay cash and don't use your real name.

According to both of my own psychics, I have gleaned Mark is at complete peace in his new environment and that he's especially proud I'm not being a Debbie Downer and moping around all over the place. "I never knew he could be such a chatterbox," one of them told me. Yeppers. That's Mark for sure. On several occasions she has had to ask him to leave her alone for a while so she could work. Happily, he always complies, saving up his chatter for the next time he senses she is free to listen.

I have, of course, asked both of them if they have any intel on why Mark keeps moving the rug. The response, they tell me, is just a chuckle. They interpret this to mean he only wants to have some fun reminding me he's around.

I've asked if he was lonely. The response is that he hasn't had time to think about it. Time, they explained, moves differently in the Hereafter. He doesn't even know he's been gone a few weeks, a few months, even a year. For him, he may only have been gone for seconds or minutes. A hard concept to wrap my head around but one which strangely gives me peace. When he was alive, he was often restless and always looking for something to do. Whatever plane he occupies is now one in which he simply *is*.

I'm told his biggest initial fear is that *I* would be the one who'd be lonely, that I'd shut myself away with only my fictional characters for daily company. During his last week in the hospital, his oncology doctor visited him regularly. In a beautiful letter he wrote me after Mark's death, he said that all Mark wanted to talk about was me and his hopes that I could be strong and soldier on. He further expressed the hope I'd find someone new so the rest of my life wouldn't be spent alone.

This made me smile and ponder how, exactly, Mark would handle that if I *did* indeed remarry. In real life, he did have a somewhat possessive, jealous streak (though not to the point as to become really annoying). Would he have been cured of this after death? If we were a television sitcom, he'd be the sort of ghost popping in at inopportune (translated: intimate) times, flailing about and shouting, "You there! What are you doing? Get your hands off my wife!"

Although my candlelight conversations with him about my day have slowly tapered off with the passage of time, I still wake up at three in the morning and wonder if he's going to dial in a message or subliminally help me work out a plot-point solution if I find I have written myself into a mental cul-de-sac. When I wake up a few hours later and discover I have somehow solved whatever problem I put out into the Universe, who's to say it wasn't Mark whispering in my ear?

I do remember one thing he told me when I asked if he had any special message about how I should be living my life. It was about "facing forward in the now." I was perplexed at first about what such fortune cookie cryptology meant and ended up asking one of my psychics if she could decipher it for me.

"Pretty simple really," she replied. "Mark's biggest fear was that if you dwell too much on the past, the world as you know it could significantly shrink. Memories that should make you smile could make you start to cry instead because they feel gone forever. You might also be sad if you dwell too much on all of the future plans you had made and travels you had hoped to enjoy. The past is done. The future is still unwritten. My message to you, ____________ (and it was here she used the nickname only I knew), is to embrace The Now, to savor all of its surprises, and to wake up each morning saying, 'I own this day and can do whatever I want with it.'"

She also said that he added, "Never give up. Never surrender." Which made me laugh. Only Mark would borrow a line from *Galaxy Quest*.

But perhaps Alan Rickman took him aside and told him to.

EMBRACING PURPOSE AND NAVIGATING LIMERENCE

"**M**aybe you've been assigned this mountain to show others it can be moved."

The author of this quote is unknown but it may as well be my own mantra about life. For as long as I can remember, I have always had a purpose which makes me excited to get up every morning. Even when those mornings involved getting dressed and going to a job which was only marginally satisfying and replete with bosses and coworkers who would someday end up as chalk outlines in my murder mysteries, I never lost sight of the fact that my purpose was to be a writer.

Over the years, I collected other quotes which reinforced the importance of knowing why I was here:

"The mystery of human existence lies not in just staying alive, but in finding something to live for." – Fyodor Dostoyevsky

"If you have a strong purpose in life, you don't have to be pushed. Your passion will drive you there." – Roy T. Bennett

"The meaning of life is to find your gift. The purpose of life is to give it away." – Pablo Picasso

"The purpose of life is to live it, to taste experience to the utmost, to reach out eagerly and without fear for newer and richer experience." – Eleanor Roosevelt

"Your work is your love made visible." – Khalil Gibran

"It's not enough to have lived. We should be determined to live for something." —Winston S. Churchill

"The person without a purpose is like a ship without a rudder." —Thomas Carlyle

"Your purpose in life is to find your purpose and give your whole heart and soul to it" — Buddha

When I began following comments on Facebook in groups which had been established for grieving widows and widowers, a common theme emerged. Those who had been married for more than half of their lives expressed that they not only felt the loss of their partner but also their own loss of a sense of purpose.

Likewise, the ladies I met in the grief support group shared stories of not knowing what to do with themselves now that they were no longer half of a couple. Marriage and children had so consumed their lives 24/7 there was little opportunity to develop outside interests, non-family connections or even hobbies. While widowhood suddenly opened a door to boatloads of free time, there was a reluctance to step through it.

"At my age," one of them said with a deep sigh of resignation, "what's the point? Whatever I start, I probably won't finish."

In my opinion, the point is that people will age all the more faster if there isn't something out there to get them up and moving and challenging their senses and sensibilities. So *what* if you don't finish the novel you start to write or the picture you start to paint or the composition you start to learn on the cello? The point is that you define a clear and manageable purpose for yourself and go out and pursue it with gusto.

It certainly doesn't have to be anything epic. Maybe your purpose is to finally organize your crafts closet. Or to train for a 5K run. Or to reconnect with old friends. Or to take a more active part in your community. As long as it gives you satisfaction, gives a positive jump start to every morning and gives you a sense of accomplishment at the end of each day, you will have found the mojo that gives your heart, body and soul the fuel it needs to keep humming.

When our friend Peter lost his beloved Lucille, he could very much have been a candidate for joining her a few weeks later. She was his world, his muse, his everything. There were, however, two factors which kept him going. The first was that Peter had a head-full of novels he had yet to write and that was his all-consuming passion and purpose. From sunrise to sundown, he was typing away in his home office. He'd be on the phone with me or sending emails asking what I thought of his latest plot. Whenever we visited the Monterey Peninsula, he could always be lured away to long lunches at Fandango and, of course, to tell us about all of the new projects he was working on.

Were I to ever script the perfect demise for Peter S. Fischer, it would be to be found face-down on his keyboard in the middle of a sentence and everyone would wonder what the rest of the sentence would have been.

The second factor is that if Peter had shown up at the Pearly Gates two weeks after Lucille, both she and his best friend Jerry would have demanded to know what he was doing there so soon. At 6'1", Jerry would likely then have grabbed Peter by the scruff of the neck, pitched him through the clouds to get back to work and gallantly escorted Lucille to dinner.

Another widower friend of mine posed the question to me of how long a time it would be appropriate to grieve. He was still working in a high-profile job, had a strong family support network and was constantly trying new hobbies to expand his mental margins. In other words, he wasn't lacking for things to do or places to be. He was also very analytical and wasn't going to settle for a response that grief didn't have a definitive timeline. "But what if it *did*?" he pressed.

Off the top of my head, I came up with Hamlett's Five Percent Theory of Grieving. He was instantly intrigued that what he was going through could be distilled to a mathematical equation.

Briefly—and mind you, I was making all of this up as I went along—a person is absolutely allowed to openly grieve as much as they want for five percent of the total duration of the relationship. This means crying, screaming, kvetching, punching pillows, being a recluse, etc. As long as you're not doing any harm to yourself or to anyone else, you are entitled to be as lost and inconsolable as you want. Once the five percent threshold has been reached, it is time to slowly return to the land of the living.

His keen analytical mind was racing. He related that since he and his wife had been together for ten years, his five percent "grieving grace period" was six months. "That's not so bad," he remarked. All right, so he may have taken my suggestion a bit too literally but it lightened his mood immensely. He could envision an end was actually in sight and that he was unilaterally allowed to be as depressed as he wanted to between now and then.

When I checked in with him six months later, he was not only happy again but was also back in the dating pool. Not long after, he even found a woman he wanted to take grand adventures with when he retired and, to this day, I never know where his next postcard will be coming from.

I've come to appreciate that my five percent theory doesn't just apply to relationships. It applies to anything which can distract us from the joys of living in the Now. Have you ever obsessed about a disappointment which occurred years ago? Perhaps the disappointment itself drained you of hope for only two weeks and yet—all of this time later—it's still festering. Under the five percent theory, two weeks is 336 hours. Accordingly, you were entitled to rage and be grumpy for—oh, hello? What's this? Only 16.8 hours? That's less than a day.

In the words of a longtime friend, "Build a bridge and get over it."

Unfortunately, sorrows of the heart cannot be dealt with so succinctly. Many women I've known who enjoyed lifetime partnerships have been content to cherish the happy memories, to commemorate the special occasions and to remind themselves on a regular basis of all the encouragement, support and nourishing they received. Now and again, a photograph, a favorite song or a whiff of cologne will bring all of the sorrow back and remind them that grief never leaves completely.

The luckiest ones are those who—happy as they were as a couple—never lost sight of themselves or their true worth as individuals. Transitioning to widowhood may have had its rough spots but their ability to embrace purpose, to seek out new opportunities and to never stop being an attentive student of life is what has made the difference between these women and the ones who sat in the grief support group and said they honestly didn't know what to do. I hope the latter eventually find their way. I hope this book can help.

I return to the quote which began this particular chapter.

"Maybe you've been assigned this mountain to show others it can be moved."

At the time of Mark's death, I already had great gobs of purpose on my plate and wasn't seeking out any more to add to it. As I began to share the stories of what I experienced, however, the idea for the book began to take form. Friends began telling me that I'd be their go-to gal at such time they lost their own spouses. (Hmm...should I add that to my business card as well?) Something about the aplomb with which I was handling everything was somehow inspiring them.

When I started doing teasers on social media about the book's development, total strangers began asking me when it was going to be on the market.

I suppose having moved my own mountain out of the way through the sheer force of winging it, who better to show others that it was indeed possible? Whether by teaspoon, shovel or bulldozer, Widowhood Mountain is only an obstacle on your path if you allow it to be.

⁕⁕⁕

I credit my sweet friend, Vicki (also a widow) with introducing me to a word I had never heard before: Limerence.

The word was first coined in the 1970s by psychologist Dorothy Tenov and describes the desire to be close to the object of one's affections, rabbit on about them constantly to friends, and being unable to stop thinking of them for more than a nanosecond.

On the surface, it sounds a lot like the early signs of love: the attraction, the pursuit, the consummation. When managed wisely and recognized for what it is, limerence can sometimes blossom into something everlasting.

The darker side of limerence is that it can become obsessive and so focus on fulfilling one's own needs that the desires of the other person get totally overlooked. If there isn't reciprocity, the anxiety of filling the void left by a dead spouse can turn angry and vengeful.

Limerence is usually short-lived depending on the grieving person's persistence to lock down a replacement. If their tactics aren't working, it's easy enough to cast their net elsewhere in pub crawling or singles groups. My own philosophy on this is that one *attracts* whatever one *projects*. If a widow or widower is desperate for companionship, s/he will either find another equally desperate soul out there or a predator who will be more than happy to prey on their insecurities and need for validation.

The creation of an emotional dependency can subsequently lead to idealizing the new person who has swanned into one's life or, worse, trying to mold them into the spitting image of the dearly departed. Seriously, there are only so many times a person can hear, "But that's not the way Fred used to do it" or have recipes foisted upon them in order to replicate meals the beloved spouse always used to make.

A grieving person can likewise try to mold themselves into what s/he believes the other person wants. Whether it's radical makeovers, incorporating hobbies and activities they don't even like, cutting themselves off from friends and family, compromising personal boundaries or values, or engaging in destructive behaviors which affect their health and well-being, attachment theory goes a long way in explaining how limerence can develop following the devastation of widowhood.

If someone has grown up in a secure, happy, nurturing environment, there's a greater likelihood of forming healthy attachments. The limerence dynamic can lead to some wonderful friendships, flirtations and even new romance.

On the flip side, someone who has had a succession of abandonment issues and rejection throughout their childhood and into adulthood will be hungrily seeking someone who can make all of the pain go away. Perhaps they found it in the spouse they just lost and are desperately hoping that lightning can strike twice or more.

The positive news is that if you are experiencing limerence, it means you still have the potential to feel love and romance intensely and on all cylinders. You just need to turn all of that energy into a positive state of self-awareness and learn to put yourself first rather than another person. Keep a journal if necessary. When you start to meet new people, write down what it is you really like and admire about them, how they make you feel about yourself and what you might learn from each other if the relationship advances.

Let go of the belief you need external validation to be a worthy and lovable individual. No one but you can solve your problems, banish your insecurities or make you feel less lonely. Ask yourself what fills you with bliss *outside* of relationships. Practice daily affirmations. Look at your platonic friendships and remind yourself of what makes these relationships so solid and fun and dependable in your life.

Is there a possibility there *won't* be someone new in this lifetime? Would you be all right with that?

In the 1970 film *On a Clear Day You Can See Forever*, a chain-smoking Daisy Gamble (played by Barbra Streisand) seeks the help of psychiatrist Marc Chabot (Yves Montand) to try to kick her habit. While under hypnotherapy, her colorful prior life emerges as a 19th century coquette and blackmailer named Lady Melinda. As their sessions continue, Marc is conflicted between his professional obligations and his growing attraction for a woman who has been dead for over a hundred years.

This, of course, does not resonate favorably with Daisy who has conflicts of her own between her kooky and laid-back ex step-brother and her engagement to a fiancé who tries to control her. Although Marc ultimately loses her at the end, she leaves him with the sweet prognostication bon mot that the two of them will have a lovely life together in the distant future. In and of itself, the anticipation he will indeed see her again is enough to leave a smile on his face.

A belief in soulmates can work two ways during the grieving process. If you believe that you and your one and only are meant to be reunited in the next lifetime, it should give you a nice sense of peace, a continuation of the love story you began together in *this* lifetime. Aside from amusing companionship or putting to good use an extra ticket to a concert, thoughts of remarriage are usually tabled and, thus, angst doesn't enter the equation. You already found your one true love and can be grateful for it, regardless of when, where and how it came to an end. One widow friend of mine described it as, "Joe just went on ahead so he can show me the ropes when I get there myself."

Conversely, fixating on the perceived perfections of the only partner you think could ever make you happy can close the door on possibilities which might have turned out to be even better. As humans, we tend to exaggerate facts and idealize those we have lost. One need only listen to eulogies which so glowingly extol the virtues of the deceased as to make the mourners feel guilty for not appreciating them more or scratch their heads and think, "Are they reading someone else's tribute by mistake?"

In the wake of someone's passing, the collective outpouring of sympathy often overwhelms any potential narrative to suggest s/he was anything less than a paragon of supreme glowy goodness. Referred to as "canonization by death," it's a phenomenon which conforms to societal expectations that we must speak well of those who can no longer speak for themselves.

Yet being able to acknowledge both the positive and negative aspects of a relationship is vital to the recovery process, especially with the passage of time. A friend of mine who lost her husband six years ago has had no shortage of respectful suitors who could lift her out of her depression and back into the land of the living. Truth be told, her late husband wasn't particularly kind to her through most of their marriage and devolved into someone even worse as his illness advanced.

Unfortunately, this hasn't dissuaded her from slavishly keeping him on a pedestal and hanging a "Keep Out" sign on her heart.

We can continue to honor the dead by remembering the qualities for which we loved and admired them but, at the same time, we must also recognize and accept their flaws. The longer posthumous adoration stays at the forefront of memory, the more it can perpetuate distortions of reality and keep the survivor from moving forward and into a happier, healthier existence.

RITUALS, ROUTINES,
REINVENTIONS AND
THE WAVE

Whether you were together for five years or fifty, it's a given that certain conventions underscored your life together. Perhaps it was the division of labor. He mowed the lawn every Saturday. You turned on the coffee and brought in the morning paper. He took out the garbage. You sent out the birthday cards to relatives. He did the taxes. You managed the finances.

Perhaps there were favorite traditions you observed. Tuesday date nights. A favorite meal to celebrate big and small accomplishments. Anniversary getaways. Decorating the Christmas tree together. Taking the grandchildren to theme parks every summer.

And now it's just you.

You having to learn to do *everything*.

The important thing to remember is that you don't have to learn to do everything all at once. If, for instance, there were holiday traditions the two of you enjoyed every November and December and it is currently only February, you don't have to start thinking about them this very instant. In fact, rituals involving other family members will likely be thought about *for* you, especially in the first year of your being alone.

Rituals have existed in all forms and across all cultures for centuries. What they have in common is a belief that performing symbolic actions prior to something that could potentially go wrong will influence a successful outcome. That they also bring a degree of predictability in an uncertain world serves to reduce anxiety. They may not make sense to anyone else but they don't have to; they only have meaning to the people doing them.

Is there any scientific basis, for instance, that the ritual of kissing your spouse goodbye as they leave for the office or kissing your children before they leave for school will keep them safe throughout the day? Absolutely not and yet we do them anyway. I recall a sweet anecdote told by Jay Leno that he always kissed his wife, Mavis, before he got in his car to drive to work. One morning he got halfway to the studio before he realized he hadn't kissed her. He immediately turned around and drove home. You know, just in case.

As a new widow, the challenge is to embrace new rituals which will imbue you with optimism and send you forth with unabashed gusto. Whether it's buying yourself fresh flowers the first week of every month, talking to your dearly departed before bedtime, putting on your lucky socks before you go for a walk, saying "thank you" every time you see a shiny penny on the ground or an iridescent hummingbird in a bush, starting each morning with your favorite song, or saying daily affirmations—these are all part of the design to make your future feel a smidge more secure.

Need some affirmations to get you started? Try these:
I will not only survive this loss but I will also thrive.
I am grateful for what we had and for what I have still.
It is okay to not be strong every single moment.
I will be happy again when I am ready.
I care for myself as much as I cared for my beloved.
I breathe in peace and breathe out sorrow.
I am stronger than I think.
I am resilient.
Every door that closes is a new door that opens.

When it comes to the workaday routines which you had grown accustomed to your partner managing, what are some of the more immediate things which come to mind and how many of them can't be put off?

Let's start with getting your cars serviced. If this was something your spouse typically handled, it's time you start learning where he took the cars and what kind of maintenance schedule they are on. This was one of the questions I had happened to ask Mark before he died. I also discovered via his email that they sent out regular service reminders. All I had to do was add them to my own calendar and request future notices be sent to me directly.

Mark had also paid the rent and the utilities every month. I might have been daunted if I hadn't done this during the times I was single. This, in turn, had given me familiarity with household budgeting. In the grief support group meetings I attended, it was apparent there were several ladies who had never had bill-paying on their regular task lists. While it does call to value the efficiency of automatic deductions being withdrawn from a checking account or charged to a credit card, it can lead to a false sense of security if a survivor has no clue what these monthly amounts are or if a payment is declined because the card has expired. As early as possible, you need to suss out the full picture.

The hugsman was a clean freak when it came to household chores such as vacuuming, dusting, and cleaning the kitchen and bathrooms. He usually made Saturday his go-to day for these activities while I did laundry whenever the basket was filled to the point of items almost spilling over. I knew that the house-cleaning needed to get done but I also knew that not only would it take me far longer than it took him but my end result also wouldn't meet his exacting standards. My solution was, thus, to research local housecleaning services and find out which one best fit my needs. I only need them once a month but having a home that absolutely sparkles is a priceless boost to my morale.

Do you like to make To Do lists? In the first weeks and months of widowhood, it can be a challenge to muster the energy to tackle much of anything. My psychic in England has employed a guaranteed dopamine burst whenever she is depressed or feeling unmotivated. Specifically, make a list of totally menial activities which are part of your daily regimen:

Brush your teeth.

Wash your face.

Take a shower.

Make coffee or tea.

Read the newspaper.

Eat breakfast.

Check your email.

Get dressed.

Make your bed.

Each time you perform one of these simple rituals, check it off your list. It's silly, she says, but there's a great sense of accomplishment in crossing things off and having a visual record that you didn't just stay under the covers all day.

Look around your environment and ask yourself whether there could be a more efficient ordering or rearrangement of items you look at all the time. In our kitchen, for example, it was Mark who had first set out the coffeemaker, blender, espresso machine, wooden knife caddy, and ceramic canister for spatulas and spoons. Whenever I wanted to make toast, I had to pull the toaster out of a lower cupboard, make the toast and then put it back again. After his death, I discovered there was a way to keep the toaster in plain sight by taking advantage of counter space not previously used.

The pantry underwent a major redesign with items I normally had to stand on a stool to reach being reassigned to lower shelves. Granted, I probably could have made these same suggestions while he was alive and he'd have been fine with it. And then, of course, forever asking me, "Where does the such-and-such live now?" The hugsman was very much a creature of habit. As am I. Except now the habits are ones I introduced to make life easier for myself.

Even the garage was subject to some switching out. When we first moved to Dobbs Mill, I parked my Miata on the left side and he parked his Passat on the right. The wisdom of this is that his car was much bigger and whenever I was a passenger, it required more room to open the passenger door. (Rarely was he a passenger in *my* car.) When I traded in the Passat for the Forester, I automatically assumed it was *supposed* to be on the right side. Another silly light-bulb moment when I realized nothing was stopping me from switching their positions and actually making it worlds easier to drive both of them in and out.

And should your own circumstances be that you are going from a two-car household down to just one, go ahead and park it right in the middle!

Did the two of you always sit in the same chairs at your dining room table? What an amazing difference it makes if you start sitting in the chair your beloved used to occupy. I had become so accustomed to seeing the same backdrop at every meal that I didn't fully appreciate the view he used to enjoy until I changed chairs.

I've also talked to a number of people who started sleeping on the opposite side of the bed. A widower friend admitted he actually took a page from actor/comedian George Burns when the latter revealed he started sleeping on Gracie's side after she passed away. The logic, as it was explained, is that he couldn't bear to see her side of the bed now empty but that it didn't bother him at all to see his own spot bare.

Reinventions of oneself don't have to be life-altering or even particularly dramatic. They are simply about creating a better version of yourself to accommodate your new outlook, new needs and new circumstances. It starts with looking at where you are in this moment and identifying what should be changed in order for you to be your happiest.

Do all of the clothes in your closet fit? Chances are there are a number of outfits you haven't worn in years or that you are hanging onto for such time as you lose weight. If you're already depressed dealing with the pressures of widowhood, the last thing you need is a wardrobe of clothes reminding you that you used to be someone else. Lay everything out. Try everything on. Discard what no longer fits or works. Celebrate the fact that donating these items will make you feel better in helping others who really need them.

Does your current lifestyle align with the goals and dreams you'd like to pursue? These include issues such as work/life balance, space requirements (stay put or downsize?), health and exercise regimens, social interactions and any bad habits or addictions you'd like to beat. Are there hobbies or new skills that could unlock your creative side or be beneficial in career advancement? Do you want to spend more quality time with your family or embrace freedom to the fullest and travel?

Invest in envisioning what your reinvented life could look like, then make a list of the steps it will take for that dream to manifest. If it helps, create a vision board and display it in a prominent place to remind yourself of what you're working toward. Identify any unhealthy habits which may be holding you back.

Lastly, a major component of reinvention is to surround yourself with the right people who know what it is you're trying to accomplish. Much too often, widows can be encumbered by all of the heavy emotional baggage that relatives and friends insist they keep carrying. While you obviously can't forget or ignore the past, it's essential that it not rigidly define your present or your future. Confidence and self-esteem are key to knowing and believing you deserve the best life has to offer.

Sure, it's easy enough to stay in one's comfort bubble and never try anything new but your whole *life* is new now. Grab it with both hands, give it a good shake and be amazed by where it can take you.

One of the first things we noticed when we moved to Dobbs Mill is that people like to wave at each other. Even total strangers. Jessica Fletcher would fit right in. In the opening credits of *Murder, She Wrote*, she is seen waving enthusiastically as she rides her bicycle through Cabot Cove.

Never, by the way, is she seen in a car unless it is as a passenger. This was a purposeful trait incorporated into the storyline. The real-life Angela Lansbury eschewed violence and thought the inclusion of a car would inevitably lead to gratuitous chases and crashes. The fictional J.B. Fletcher had simply never learned to drive. (Up until the age of 30, yours truly hadn't learned to drive, either, but was taught over the course of two weekends by an actor friend and subsequently passed my test with flying colors.)

The hugsman and I had never before lived in a place where waving was such a popular form of greeting. If you're driving in a parking lot and reach an intersection at the same time as another driver, the odds are high s/he will smile, wave and insist you go first. Even pedestrians who have the right of way will take this moment to wave you through or wave in appreciation that you let them cross. Walking the dog and seeing another dog-walker in the next block will also be cause to wave. The first time I did that, Mark asked me if it was someone I knew.

"No," I replied, "but they seem nice enough."

Once someone starts, it's a happy practice that continues even if you never pass close enough to exchange names or have a conversation. Additionally, it makes every trip to a store take ten minutes longer than it should because of all the "You-go-ahead-no-no-I-think-you-were-first-but-really-I- insist" gestures of kindness which prevail in a part of the world which is just so darned nice.

Whether you continue to live where you are or move to someplace new, start incorporating waves into your out-and-about ritual and see how good it makes you feel. Plus you can imagine someone's companion saying, "Is that someone you know?" And them replying, "No, but she seems nice."

And it's because you are.

THE HELPMATES

Between 1978 and 1986, I ran my own touring theatre company. This not only required me to wear many hats—writing, acting, directing, producing, holding auditions, budgeting, marketing—but also seduced me into the trap of believing I actually *had* to do all of those things.

Now and again I'd get frazzled and someone would say, "Do you need some help with that?" Rather than graciously accept the offer, my immediate response was always, "No, no, I've got this. Thanks anyway."

I blame it on an upbringing which dictated that accepting help to do something was somehow an admission of weakness and failure.

Long after I disbanded the acting company to focus on my writing, the habit of saying "no" was still going strong. In our married life, Mark would often see me struggling with a jar lid or trying to carry too many grocery bags or getting frustrated with my computer and he'd ask if I needed help. Even when common sense told me he could "fix" whatever it was faster than I could, it was almost as if I had to continually prove I was strong and self-sufficient.

Upon reflection, I recall a number of friendships where I was reluctant to accept favors because it would only be a matter of time I'd be called upon to respond in turn. What if I was too busy? What if it was something I really didn't want to do? How would this potentially tie me to someone I didn't want to be tied to?

Likewise, I was reluctant to seek out assistance because it might project I was needy or vulnerable. What sort of awkwardness might ensue if I had misread the parameters of our relationship? What if they said "no"?

As a society I think we *underestimate* the willingness of others to lend a hand just as much as we *overestimate* how inconvenienced, put-upon and put-out our request might make them feel. As aggressively as we are taught throughout our lives to be autonomous, so, too, have we been taught to view with suspicion anyone who cheerfully rushes in to be a helpmate.

"What's their angle?" we think. "What are they expecting out of this?" "Are they just trying to get close in order to harm me?" "What's their real agenda?"

Whether we have a fear of strings attached or letting go of some measure of control, we're actually robbing ourselves of opportunities for social connection. In reality, we all feel warm and fuzzy when we have done something which lightens the load of another person. Why should we not give them the same opportunity and let them help us as well?

When we moved to Dobbs Mill in 2021, neither one of us knew anyone here. We both had no shortage of friends across the country and even around the world. Technology certainly made it easy to stay in touch with all of them. We thoroughly enjoyed each other's company and were happy to spend 24/7 together. But is that really enough?

Following his Stage 4 cancer diagnosis, Mark emphasized the importance of my making new friends in our community. Easier said than done, I think. A bit like transferring to a new high school in your senior year. All of the cliques have already been formed and it's just too hard for an outsider to successfully break in with the popular kids.

Both of us were naturally gregarious and always chatting up grocery checkers, store owners, restaurateurs and wait staff. We knew all of them by name and he felt it would just be a short leap for me to start making coffee and lunch dates. I also feel that dog owners have an advantage in that there's always a chat involved when you're walking your respective pooches. (Although oftentimes I knew the dogs' names before I ever learned the names of their owners.)

The other promise the hugsman extracted from me is that if anyone—upon learning my new circumstances—should offer to help, I should smile and take them up on it.

"But what if I can't think of anything?" I asked him.

He smiled and said, "Then thank them and tell them you'll take them up on their offer just as soon as something comes to mind."

When neighbors happened to ask whether my husband had lost weight ("Has he been going to the gym?"), I bit the bullet and told them truthfully what was really going on. The outpouring of love and support was far beyond what I had expected. "Knock on our door anytime," they offered, "and we'll be there for you."

During the grueling trips back and forth to St. Luke's, I asked our management office if they would mind looking after Lucy during the day. I do believe she got more walks out of them than she had from me because they were so excited to have a dog to play with and fuss over!

Almost overnight, our next door neighbor became one of my closest friends and encouraged me to call her if I ever felt like a good cry or just talking.

Two other neighbors of mine were instrumental in helping me trade in Mark's car for a vehicle that would be more suitable for winter weather than my low-to-the-ground Miata.

Our jeweler has become like a trusted sister and is always up for brunching and lunching.

My favorite cashier at the grocery store makes a point of coming around and giving me a hug every time I'm at her checkstand.

And when one of the ladies from the grief support group asked me what I was doing for Thanksgiving and I said I'd just be home with Lucy, she responded, "No, you're not. You're coming to *our* house. You'll fit right in with all of our crazy relatives!" On top of that, she even offered her cozy guest room so I wouldn't have to drive home by myself on a dark and stormy night.

The abundance of warmth you can find when you have the courage to reach out for it reminds me of Hugh Grant's voiced monologue at the opening of my favorite Christmas movie:

"If you look for it," he says, "I've got a sneaky feeling you'll find that love, actually, is all around."

It truly is.

And I have been blessed to find so much of it in the midst of losing all that I held dear.

CAPTAIN OF MY HEART

Although the title of this book is an appreciative nod to J.B. Fletcher, she is not the only fictional widow from whom I drew inspiration and optimism in my first months of widowhood.

In 1968, a television series debuted called *The Ghost and Mrs. Muir*, an adaptation of a much loved film of the same name starring Rex Harrison and Gene Tierney. The setting is Schooner Bay, Maine, and the premise is that a young widow (Hope Lange) with two small children agrees to rent a charming house called Gull Cottage.

They are initially unaware their new home already has a resident, its original owner named Captain Daniel Gregg (Edward Mulhare), who has been haunting it for over a century. Only when he decides to make his presence known in an effort to scare them away is the groundwork laid for a fractious coexistence replete with sensual chemistry.

Minus the enchantment of singing and dancing furniture to keep him company, he is very much a (*Beauty and the*) *Beast* who hasn't realized there is only one thing which can set him free and allow him to find the happiness and sense of belonging which has so aggressively eluded him in both Life and the Hereafter.

Old World chauvinism and Modern Woman sensibilities quickly collide. Can a romance between Carolyn Muir and Daniel be far behind? Did I mention Carolyn supported her family in this seaside sanctuary by being a successful writer who—like J.B.

Fletcher—composed her work on a Royal manual typewriter? And that she has an impossibly cute and scene-stealing little dog?

I guess the only other question is why Maine attracts fictional female wordsmiths navigating their way through widowhood, living in fabulously well-furnished houses and looking stylish the entire time.

Carolyn and Jessica have something else in common. They both continued to wear their wedding rings throughout the duration of their respective series. As do I. As a matter of fact, I had Mark's amethyst wedding ring resized for my own finger and intend to keep wearing it until such opportunity as it is replaced by something else.

And yes, it also makes an effective deterrent against unwelcome advances.

I was still in high school when *The Ghost and Mrs. Muir* debuted but what wasn't to love about the swoonworthy Captain or to admire about the self-confident widow? I had by and large set these remembrances aside for five decades until my own Captain very much materialized in the form of someone Mark and I had both known for 16 years.

Although I had met him first and struck up a casual friendship, the three of us soon began planning get-togethers for lunches and dinners. I admit I didn't pay much attention at the start but these two men completely enjoyed each other's company, respective senses of humor, political repartee and smart conversation.

They also both adored me, and yet our companion—long divorced—would never have done or said anything inappropriate, ours being a marriage he deeply admired and respected. He knew the background of our courtship, too, and opined it was one of the most romantic true stories he had ever heard.

Even after we moved to another state in 2021, Mark was often the first to propose Zoom meetings so we could all catch up on news. I recall several of our conversations involved a future trip Mark and I wanted to take to Portugal.

"Hey, you know who might be fun to invite along?" Mark said after one of our Zooms.

In our entire marriage, this was the only time he had ever entertained the idea of having company. He teased the idea of our friend donning a white dinner jacket and playing piano bar at Reid's Palace, our destination of choice.

"Sounds like it's not too early for me to start practicing," our friend quipped.

I, in turn, began studying Portuguese so I could be the lads' savvy translator.

This wonderful man was not as yet my Captain but he was on the long list of people I contacted after Mark passed away. He was among the first to reach out and ask if there was anything he could do, even at a distance.

"I don't know," I said, because I really didn't. "Maybe check in on me once a week?"

Doubtful I'd become like our widow friend who spent much of the first year drunk on her kitchen floor and eating cookies. More likely, he'd be getting my answering machine while I swanning off doing something interesting and brunching with friends.

I'm not entirely sure how he ended up making our phone dates at seven every Saturday evening. I do remember I teased him about Saturdays being a traditional hot date night for people who were single. His sweet response was that there was no one he'd rather be having a hot date with on a Saturday night than me.

We talked about anything, everything, nothing. Despite 16 years of friendship, there was a lot we didn't know about each other. He encouraged me to tell him Mark stories and listened thoughtfully on the occasions some of those stories dribbled into tears. He gave me advice—but only when I requested it—and not only began reading my novels and plays but was also enthusiastic to talk about them afterward. With each passing week, I found I was looking more and more forward to Saturday evenings.

It never entered my mind our relationship would ever be more than friendship, especially since there was not only a multitude of miles between us but also a remaining three years of commitment to his employer. I suppose what hovered most in the back of my mind was the risk of *losing* the friendship if a tested romance didn't work out. While I didn't consider myself "on the market' in the dating pool, I certainly couldn't blame him if he found it appealing to date women who at least lived in his same time-zone and/or zip code.

One Friday afternoon in early summer, he called to ask me if I'd mind having that week's phone call on Sunday instead of Saturday.

"No problem," I replied. "What's up?"

He told me he had a date.

I forced a fake cheeriness into my voice and told him that sounded really, really great. Really. All right, who am I kidding? After I hung up, I asked myself why my cheeriness had been forced at all. Shouldn't I be happy for him? Maybe whoever it was would turn out to be The One. Yay.

That was probably the defining moment when I realized a part of me was jealous he'd be spending a Saturday evening in person with someone else instead of an hour or two on the phone with me. I almost contemplated not answering the phone when he called on Sunday. Make him think I was on a date of my own. Hahahahaha. I know—pretty sophomoric, wasn't it?

Instead I answered on Sunday and, in a cheery voice, asked him how his date went.

"She was nice enough," he casually replied. "But she wasn't you."

Our subsequent conversations began to take on a level of flirtation which hadn't previously existed. They also became more serious, more introspective, more trusting...and more frequent. Endearments such as "darling," "Babe" and "luv"—which sometimes felt accidental—soon became the norm and proved not to be accidental at all.

He asked if I'd like to come for a visit. I countered by reminding him that planes flew in both directions. "Hmm...so when should we do this?" he asked.

And that's when my old-fashioned sensibilities kicked in.

When the hugsman passed away, I promised myself I would adhere to the Victorian code of mourning; specifically, waiting one year before entertaining any ideas of a future romance. I think the Victorians were very smart in this. It is not only a full year to keep from rushing headlong into impractical encumbrances but also to prevent one from doing stupid things like getting tattoos, joining a nunnery, getting scary haircuts, engaging in risky sports, etc.

I would not, of course, carry the whole Victorian mourning bit to the levels of Queen Victoria who had her servants lay out the late Prince Albert's clothes every day and bring hot water for his shave. She also wore black for the remaining forty years of her life. Stylish and slimming as black can be, I'm afraid all of the colorful ensembles and accessories in my closet would feel woefully neglected if I ceased wearing them.

To me, the idea of a one-year mourning period was an easy promise to make because I really had no intention of ever dating again, much less committing myself to another marriage. The world has changed radically from my early dating days in my 20s and 30s. I seriously believe the percentage of flakes, snakes and players out there has increased. Even though technology has made it possible to separate the wheat from the chaff, it has also made the flakes, snakes and players more savvy in disguising the truth.

Yet here I was entertaining possibilities of another chapter, another happily ever after.

That, herein, presented a conundrum I had never considered; specifically, what would everyone say about it?

Many of Mark's friends and business colleagues had only ever known me as Mark's wife. They all knew I'd had an interesting life before I met him and yet weren't able to fathom how I could possibly have a life *without* him, albeit as a successful author and playwright Even friends of mine—well intentioned in their sympathy—said things like, "How hard it must be for you now to be only half a person."

Half a person? What? I'm pretty sure I actually became *quadruple* the person I was previously for all of the new challenges I had to take on in his absence. Everyone's expectation, I think, was that I would remain a glam but lonely widow, Mark's shoes being entirely too big for any mere mortal to ever fill.

"There will never be anyone else like him again," they told me.

That is certainly true. But it's not to say we can't have more than one person in a lifetime who can bring us unabashed joy and an exciting reason to get up every morning.

The friends I found most accepting of the secret I shared were those who had known Mark only marginally or, in some cases, not at all. I was the one they knew and had come to love and, for them, my being happy and being treated well by someone who loved me in return was all that was important to them. Their collective advice? Go for it, girl. You deserve it.

I decided to put the question to the one person who knew me better than anyone else.

October 17th was the 29th anniversary of when Mark and I first met. I decided to make this auspicious date the focal point of my trip to British Columbia and my stay at the Fairmont Empress. Since we had intended to enjoy High Tea at the Palm Court, I called in early May to make my reservations. "I hope I'm not calling too soon," I said. I was told my timing was actually perfect since Fall was already starting to fill up.

Thank goodness I didn't wait until the day before; they might have apologized and handed me a tea bag to take back to my room!

Several acquaintances expressed astonishment that I was not only taking a trip by myself but that I was also *leaving the country*. Heavens! For me, it was a personal Rubicon which needed crossing. If I could be that bold to venture solo after six months, I could probably do anything.

The morning of the 17th was cold and drizzling. I had already scattered some of Mark's ashes around the hotel grounds and at Butchart Gardens. All that remained was to walk out to Victoria Harbor, cast some ashes into the sea and ask him to give me a sign that he approved of the new romance which had entered my life.

When I arrived for High Tea, there was an older lady at the grand piano. She smiled and nodded at me as I walked in and then began to play a piece which one typically doesn't expect in the repertoire of a musician supplying tea room ambience. The moment I heard the first notes, I knew Mark had been paying attention and was quietly telling me "yes."

As if I needed any further proof, my server brought two champagne flutes to my table and set the second one down opposite me.

"Oh, I'm just here by myself," I hastily explained.

He gave me a gracious smile and a knowing wink. "It is for your husband," he replied.

Now and again I catch myself wondering whether the Captain had been sent to serve as nothing more than a pleasant distraction, that by the time I got over my grieving, our affection for one another would have waned and we would simply go back to being friends. What I couldn't seem to disguise, though, was what I was subconsciously projecting to everyone who saw me.

"Have you done something different with your hair?" they started asking. "Trying a different makeup?" "Have I ever seen you in that color before?" "Whatever you've been doing, you look amazing!"

Compliments abounded that I was looking radiant, glowing, relaxed and totally happy. Slowly but surely I came to realize that the changes they perceived in me were coming from the inside out, that optimism had taken root in my heart and had no intention of leaving any time soon.

The rational side of me can explain insofar as my outward appearance that it could have just been the dropping away of stress, worry and frustration which had defined the months leading up to Mark's death. Makeup can only do so much in terms of covering tears and lack of sleep. While no one would have faulted me if I had chosen to go days without doing my hair or face or schlepping around in wrinkled clothes, Mark himself would have been the first to say I didn't engage in any of those habits even on occasions when I was sick.

Nor would I have left the house in anything less than outfits I'd have felt comfortable having my picture taken in. Isn't it a fact that if you're dressed like a mess, there is a high likelihood you'll run into everyone you know (including former boyfriends) or that you'll be a witness to something which will invite the presence of a camera crew? Mark and I used to laugh at programs in which workaday folks who stridently claimed to have seen UFOs were never well dressed. Had extraterrestrials ever seen me, I'm sure they would have deemed there was hope for Earth after all.

But I digress...

Without my aggressively seeking it, Romance had found me and I was happy to let it. The deeper my relationship with the Captain grew, however, the more I found myself worrying about how such news might be received if and when I decided to share it. There are those who would be aghast to learn I was being respectfully courted only four months after I had decanted Mark's ashes into the champagne bottle.

Others—upon learning I had known my new beau as a friend for 16 years—might raise eyebrows in speculation something must have been clandestinely afoot during that timeframe.

It's the latter who would anger me the most and do a disservice to the integrity of all three of us. I had always believed Mark possessed more honor and integrity than anyone I had ever met. Little did I know there were *two* such men who walked the planet and that I'd be blessed enough to be cherished by both.

So what would Jessica Fletcher do?

As a successful author who owned her own home and was well liked in her community, I'm sure it was never her quest to rush out and find a replacement for her beloved Frank. Eagle eyes might have spotted their framed picture in her home (but not figured out it was actually a photo of Angela Lansbury's real-life husband). She didn't need someone to support her financially, nor did she have any children with whom a swain would have to pass critical approval. She occasionally referenced Frank in conversation and yet she kept herself open to pleasant and interesting companionship. Several of her potential admirers were demonstrably wealthy, charismatic and clearly besotted with her.

The fact she invariably figured out her dinner date's connection to the latest Cabot Cove crime and had to have him arrested by dessert, however, would only have affirmed she really was much better off by herself.

Carolyn Muir was much younger and had two young children and a dog. She rented—not owned—Gull Cottage, and money seemed to be on ongoing issue insofar as the expense of household repairs. At one point she even takes a job at the local newspaper (with a doofy Richard Dreyfuss as her editor) to supplement her income. To my knowledge, she never mentioned her late husband until an episode when his parents showed up for a visit, nor are there any photographs of him except in a locket glimpsed only briefly by Captain Gregg.

While Carolyn's in-laws might have wanted her to find someone to help raise Candy and Jonathan, how could they not have avoided comparisons to a much-loved son?

Like J.B. Fletcher, Carolyn was open to dressing up and going out on dates. The difference, of course, was the mischievous intervention of a certain ghost with a jealous streak and the steely determination there would never be a second date after the first one. Vexed as she'd get with his meddling, though, I believe she figured out early on that his rakish persona would be the benchmark against whom she'd always compare any potential suitors who were still among the living. Plus the fact he waltzed so beautifully.

While I've forged an obvious kinship with both women piloting their way through the modern waters of widowhood, Mrs. Muir's was clearly the more complicated life. Beyond her housekeeper and her children, who could she talk to openly about Captain Gregg, much less explain that the chance for her friends to meet him in person might never happen?

Time and distance may currently be on our own side in assuring we didn't rush into anything mindlessly stupid but I'm sure it may also have crossed the minds of my select circle that I had made up this magnificent man as insurance they'd never try to hook me up with someone to assuage my loneliness. I am, after all, a consummate storyteller and romantic. He may as *well* be a ghost for as enigmatic and yet ongoing a presence as he is in my life.

"Can we at least see a picture of him?" they continue to press.

My response is always a cryptic smile and leaving them to imagine the portrait of a dashing sea captain above the mantle. He has met his match in me and I in him.

For now, does anyone really need to know anything more?

I think not.

ABOUT THE AUTHOR

Former actress and theatre director Christina Hamlett is an award-winning author whose credits to date include 50 books, 271 plays, and squillions of articles, interviews and blogs. She is also a script consultant for stage and screen, a distance learning instructor in playwriting, screenwriting and cozy mysteries, a photographer and a gourmet chef. Learn more at www.authorhamlett.com.

And yes, the story of Diavlo and the champagne bottle is absolutely true.

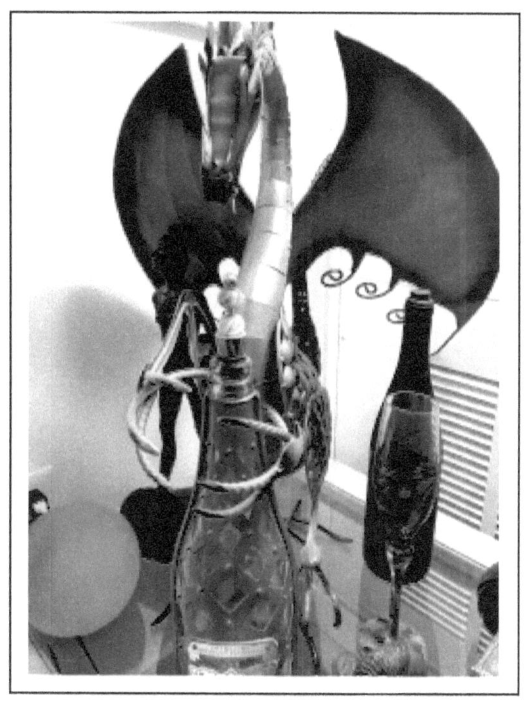

HELPFUL RESOURCES FOR YOUR JOURNEY

Now With You, Now Without: My Journey Through Life and Loss by Kathryn Leigh Scott

---

It Must Have Been Moonglow: Reflections on the First Years of Widowhood by Phyllis Greene

---

Widow To Widow: Thoughtful, Practical Ideas For Rebuilding Your Life by Genevieve Davis Ginsburg

---

Future Widow: Losing My Husband, Saving My Family, and Finding My Voice by Jenny Lisk

---

Heartbroken: Healing from the Loss of a Spouse by Gary Roe

Finding Love After Loss: A Relationship Roadmap for Widows by Marti Benedetti and Mary A. Dempsey

Good Grief: A Companion for Every Loss by Granger E. Westberg

Farewell: Vital End-of-Life Questions with Candid Answers by Edward T. Creagan, MD

Newly Widowed, Now Socially Awkward: Facing Interpersonal Challenges After Loss by Eileen L Cooley, Ph.D

Everything You Need to Know When I'm Gone - End of Life Planner for Affairs and Last Wishes by Ava Brinley

Healing After Loss: Daily Meditations For Working Through Grief by Martha Whitmore Hickman

The Five Invitations: Discovering What Death Can Teach Us About Living Fully by Frank Ostaseski

Also by Christina Hamlett

Book 1

A Little Larceny in Lynmouth

Book 2

A Little Scandal in St. Andrews

Book 3

A Little Drama in Dunster

Book 4

A Little Poison in Paisley

Book 5

A Little Tumble in Tintagel

Watch for more at www.authorhamlett.com.